NEW SENSATIONS
FOR HORSE AND RIDER

Introducing Voice Training

Tanya Larrigan

J. A. Allen

British Library Cataloguing-in-Publication Data.
A catalogue record for this book is available from the British Library.

ISBN 0.85131.767.7

Published in Great Britain in 2000 by
J. A. Allen
an imprint of Robert Hale Ltd.,
Clerkenwell House,
45–47 Clerkenwell Green,
London, EC1R OHT

Reprinted 2000

Typeset by Textype Typesetters, Cambridge
Colour separartion by Tenon & Polert Colour Scanning Ltd
Printed by Dah Hua International Printing Press Co. Ltd., Hong Kong
Designed by Nancy Lawrence
Illustrated by Maggie Raynor

This book is dedicated to three very special people:

My parents

Marion and Peter Larrigan
who have passed the knowledge on to me. Age has not made me any less impulsive
but thank you both for the encouragement in whatever venture I decide on

and

to the memory of a very dear friend
who treated all beings as equals and
gave me so much encouragement for this book –

Lady Linda McCartney

Indian Summer – my all-time favourite – we had many New Sensations, he was a horse before his time.

CONTENTS

	page
Acknowledgements	ix
Foreword by Sir Paul McCartney	xi
Introducing the horses in the book	xii
Introduction	xv
Part 1 The start for life at any age	**1**
Do you speak the same language?	2
Do you have his trust?	2
Do you respect each other?	7
What do you want from him?	11
What does he need from you?	14
Can your horse bend, will he move away from pressure?	18
How many natural and artificial aids do you use?	20
Part 2 Get started with liberty and voice training	**23**
Introduction	24
Can my horse or pony learn voice training and liberty work?	28
Lesson 1 The equipment and how to use it	30
Lesson 2 Getting ready for work	34
Lesson 3 Basic exercises explained	40
Lesson 4 Progressing with your voice and lunge work	48
Lesson 5 He is going well, now he works free	58
Lesson 6 Educating and stimulating – progressing into freestyle	63

CONTENTS

Part 3   Get started with long reining   **71**

Introduction   72
Lesson 7   Safety first   75
Lesson 8   Tack and its correct fitting   76
Lesson 9   From one to two reins   78
Lesson 10   Preliminary work with two reins   80
Lesson 11   Progressing with two-rein work on the circle   86
Lesson 12   Where to stand for long reining   88
Lesson 13   Going large on the long reins   89
Lesson 14   Useful exercises on the flat   93
Lesson 15   Introducing lateral work   97

Part 4   Get started with driving   **107**

Introduction   108
Lesson 16   What is needed to get started?   110
Lesson 17   Parts of the harness and trap   112
Lesson 18   Preparing your horse for harness   119
Lesson 19   Preparing for putting to   124
Lesson 20   Your preparation for driving   130
Lesson 21   Putting to and your first drive   133

Part 5   Get started with Western riding   **139**

Introduction   140
Lesson 22   What is needed to get started?   144
Lesson 23   Parts of the Western tack   147
Lesson 24   Tack fitting and tacking up   151
Lesson 25   Mounting your horse and the rider's position   155
Lesson 26   The gaits   161
Lesson 27   The basics of Western riding   164
Lesson 28   Exercises and trail work   171

Vocabulary   188
Useful Addresses   190

ACKNOWLEDGEMENTS

I have led an amazing and interesting life. I was born into a circus family and rode before I could walk. From a very early age I learnt that if I wanted anything from my parents it would be after the horses were done. Both my parents are quite simply fantastic when it comes to the riding, training and understanding of horses. They are acknowledged by all who know them as gifted but in different ways. My mother will analyse the problem, then remove it; she is also a brilliant trainer of riders. My father is another matter and does not analyse problems – quite simply because for him they do not exist! Some have called him a 'horse whisperer' but he does not like that label and the family and close friends call him 'Dr Dolittle' because he communicates with all animals. I owe my attitude and understanding of horses to these two people.

I have kept many friends from those early days and they do not judge on where you come from but on you the person and what you do. One man I will never forget is the late John Chipperfield whose knowledge of training and understanding horses was second to none. My parents worked with him for many years. The last time I saw him he pulled out a copy of *Horse & Hound* and pointed to a picture of me riding a lap of honour with Salute, who was attempting to take off with me. His only comment was 'your hands are too high!' I tried to explain that it was just at that moment that they went up. 'No excuses' he replied. He was a very tough taskmaster on humans but never the horses. When I told him of my ambitions he smiled and said 'you can do and achieve anything you want – it would be rather good to have a circus girl in the dressage teams'.

Really another book is needed for all the animals and the stories that went with them. Everyone of them was a friend and taught me something – even if it was how to sit a dirty buck! We could only afford problem horses and even my top ones had a hiccup. Three names stand out in my mind. The first is my mother's high school horse Rainbeau. Along with my mother he was one of my main trainers and when I was eight years old they had me riding Grand Prix and high school work. If my aids were too strong he would let me know in no uncertain manner! It was Rainbeau who took me into the dressage arena when I was eighteen and we competed in the British Team at the first Junior European Dressage Championships which were held in Aachen in 1973. The second horse is Indian Summer. I was his last chance and

we had many 'discussions' in the early days but developed the most incredible partnership. Together we did just about every discipline we could, including working on television and going back to the circus for a Christmas season as a high school act. The boy who brought me into the senior dressage big time was the third horse, Salute. Fortunately for me he was the horse nobody wanted. Let's say he had a few quirks!

Without the help of the following people my life would have taken a very different route — perhaps back to the circus permanently. I do not think that I will ever lose the grease-paint or the wanderlust that are in my blood. Following my first dressage test Domini Morgan advised me to keep going and gave me pointers in the right direction. Sigrid Young offered me Salute (even though he was a real character!) when I was about to give the dressage scene a permanent miss and return to the circus. In 1994 I thought my career was over because of serious back trouble but thanks to Mr John O'Brien, who performed major works on my lower back, I expect to hold out for another forty years!

To those of you who helped in the beginning, without whom the New Sensations training days and the Roadshows would not have happened, I say a special thank you. All the ideas in the world are fine but sometimes you need muscle and friends.

About half way through this work my father had a near fatal car crash. Thank you Caroline for giving me the extra time to finish this book.

I am amazingly lucky that I can do the work I love and it takes me all over the world meeting so many different people and animals. Closer to home, many years ago and through training horses our paths crossed with Sir Paul and Lady Linda McCartney. I was honoured when Lin agreed to write the foreword for this book because she would never agree to something she did not believe in. I, however, was late finishing and God called early. Thank you Paul for writing the piece.

Photographs have been supplied by Frank Noon, Bob Atkins, Bob and Brenda Hedley and by courtesy of *Your Horse* Magazine and Intervet UK Ltd.

FOREWORD

SIR PAUL McCARTNEY

My wife Linda was 'horse mad'. From an early age she fell in love with these noble creatures, and never looked back. She would tell me to think of them as 'big puppy dogs who allow us to ride on their back'. Like puppies, she explained, they loved to be pampered, loved, and talked to in a reassuring tone of voice.

As a child she had never owned her own horse, so I was lucky to be the one to buy her her first horse, a beautiful chestnut mare named Cinnamon.

As the years went by, we began to feel the need for a good horse trainer who would be sympathetic to our methods. Through a friend's wife we found the Larrigans – Tanya, her mother Marion, and father Peter, and soon realised that they fitted our requirements exactly. Their approach stressed one thing – kindness. If the horses were to be travelled, the trailer never went above thirty miles an hour. They were never treated roughly and were shown respect and, above all, kindness.

The methods used by Tanya and her family, who became great friends of ours, have been learned and developed through years of experience and I am so pleased that Tanya has finally taken the plunge and written them down

for future generations of riders to benefit from.

Linda had agreed to write the foreword to this excellent book, but sadly that was not to be, so I am proud to do the honours.

The techniques described in these pages are of value to all riders – from the youngest novice to the most experienced. There is always something to learn.

I will always be indebted to Linda for introducing me to the fine art of horsemanship, and similarly to the Larrigan family for making it all seem so easy.

The lessons to be learned from this book also offer clues as to how we as humans might behave in the future – with love and kindness to each other, and with respect for all the beautiful creatures we are lucky enough to share this planet with.

Happy trails!

INTRODUCING

THE HORSES IN THE BOOK

Jack 16hh six-year-old Andalucian gelding whom I have owned since he was two years old. He is riden English and Western, features in our demonstrations doing long reining and introducing the voice training with the liberty work. He is learning high school work but I am also developing his programme into a comedy display.

Hercules 31 inch (79cm) American Miniature Horse stallion aged fourteen. Hercules has been with me since he was three years old, and has worked all over the country in our demos. He has raised much monies for charities and featured with Salute as part of the *Long and the Short of It* comedy long-reining display at the Olympia Christmas show. He now leads the Mini Marvels[R] long-reining display team and featured at the European Dressage Championships with the team.

Hans 16.2hh twelve-year-old Hanoverian whom I have owned since he was four years old. He takes part in the Western demonstrations being ridden with no saddle or bridle. He is learning high school and does do higher level dressage but because of a foot problem cannot compete.

Cobber 14.2hh total mixed variety, sadly now deceased but he was with me for twenty-five years. I was given him when I was nine and my parents said that he was good value for money and would last for a few years. The only problem was that I could not reach the stirrup from the floor. If I let it down long enough then I could not get my leg over the saddle! I devised a clever way to get up. Not for me the mounting block – that was for the 'oldies' – I would put some food on the floor and Cobber would drop his head down to eat. As I scratched his neck I would lean over his neck and say 'up'. When he put his head up I could slide back to the withers and into the saddle.

Floribunda 14.2hh Appaloosa mare in training. Owned and bred by Paul and Linda McCartney.

Goliath 28¾ inch (73cm) miniature eight-year-old stallion who has been with me since he was four. He is part of the Mini Marvels[R] team and he also features in the demonstrations showing the advanced long reining with Hercules.

Rainbeau 16.2hh Thoroughbred who passed on at twenty-five years of age. An amazing character, he was my mother's high school

display horse working at Grand Prix level dressage. He and my other horses kept my feet on the ground any time I thought I was getting pretty good. All animals are great levellers!

Salute 16.2hh Swedish bred passed on at twenty-two. We were lucky to meet each other – in our first dressage test, no mark was higher than a three! Together we achieved my dreams although that is not to say there was no heartache. As well as competing at the highest level including being on the Olympic squads for Moscow and Los Angeles we travelled the country working at many different venues doing the then unheard of dressage to music displays! One of my dreams had been to work at the Olympic Christmas show and one week before the show in 1980 the Police Horse Team went down sick and the late Raymond Brooks-Ward said to me 'now is your chance, make it special'. I did not bother with the topper and tails. I raided my display wardrobe. I will not forget the feeling when the curtains went back and the lights went up on us. I still have the full length green velvet dress with gold braiding, and Salute was wearing a *diamanté* bridle and breastplate. What a feeling. The crowd loved it – he was always the showman.

Indian Summer 16.2hh Irish bred coloured with spots. He was with me for twenty-seven years and passed on when he was thirty-two. We had a great partnership competing in one-day events, grade A jumping, and he won the National Dressage Title with me in my last year as a Junior. I have never really met another like him.

Tom Tom 31 inch (85cm) miniature four-year-old, gelding, home-bred son of Hercules, working in the Mini Marvels[R] team.

Boysie 31 inch (85cm) miniature four-year-old gelding, home-bred son of Hercules, part of the Mini Marvels[R] team.

Bambi 30 inch (76cm) miniature four-year-old home-bred daughter of Goliath, part of the Mini Marvels[R] team.

Dandy 13hh Exmoor passed on at thirty-four. One of our riding school ponies who taught everyone patience and tact – the more you kicked the slower he went.

Idolo 17hh Lusitano stallion eight-year-old former circus horse owned by Mrs Cawley. He is with me for training and to compete in dressage. Takes part in our demonstrations with high school displays and Western. He is a stunner!

Illustre 15.2hh Andalucian thirteen-year-old stallion sent for dressage training by Mrs P. Rolph. We have competed together internationally and he has been in our demonstrations showing Western work.

Danny 16.2hh home-bred six-year-old gelding out on loan to a friend to enjoy life. We have decided not to breed or sell anymore. We feel there are enough people in the world doing that but there is a need for welfare promotion.

Vinnie 16.1hh home-bred six-year-old gelding. He is an interesting character, not really mellowing with age but learning to handle life.

Sparky 31 inch (85cm) miniature accident! Two-year-old son of Goliath who found a rail down into the ladies' field.

Embassy Twenty-four-year-old Thoroughbred

who was rescued as a weaving yearling colt locked in a stable. He has been a training horse and had a revolutionary hock operation which was a success.

Diplomat Twenty-four-years-old. One of my former top dressage horses. We were on the long list for the Seoul Olympics, but my back kept us out of contention for the Barcelona Games. Now teaching a friend's husband Western!

Swop 13hh passed on at thirty-six. She came as a Christmas present when I was seven. A Welsh cross and not the prettiest but beauty is in the eyes of the beholder. Amongst other things I used to ride down to the village shop on her and tie her up outside to get the groceries.

Laddie 16hh Thoroughbred home-bred gelding, passed on when twenty-five-years old. He suffered a fracture when racing and he was the first horse that I trained for liberty work. He

joined in on the demonstrations and I used him to show another side of training. He also loosened the audience up, because he did not always do as he was asked!

Snowy 16hh seven-year-old Thoroughbred mare. She has been with us since she was a two-year-old and is now proven on the flat and over hurdles. I used to ride racehorses in the States so we did a lot of work on her before she went into training. It paid off and I have a dream of riding her in a ladies' race. Now home, she will start to learn Jack's programme.

Warrior four-year-old 30 inch spotted stallion who came from The Tanzivan Stud as a two-year-old. He is part of the Mini Marvel[R] team and I will be showing him.

Racing Camels They came from Longleat Lion Reserve. Dad trained and travelled them around the country for shows and other venues.

INTRODUCTION

For many years I have thought about writing a book but I was thinking along the lines of a Jilly Cooper type – bedtime reading set in the dressage world. It would have been very interesting and I would have had to use lots of imagination! Yet those literary plans and dreams were put on hold following an event in 1997.

As a rider and trainer I have always been of the opinion that variety is the key word when working horses. However, one day whilst having lunch with Lesley, an editor friend, we were discussing reader offers and I pointed out that magazines all seemed to offer the same type of thing. After throwing ideas around and knowing that I could not get my dessert until I had offered something very different I came up with the following suggestion. What if I could put together a package that offered the readers a variety of disciplines which they could try in an informal, relaxed atmosphere? All the people had to do was come to us. We would supply all the horses, little and large. There would only be ten each day and this way everyone would integrate more easily. Lunch would give them time to have a breather and discuss their morning antics followed by an afternoon session. The groups would first watch me working through the programmes, and then be divided between my parents and me so that they could have a go at the different disciplines. The idea behind my thinking was to keep the pressure off everyone, so that no one had to try anything they did not want to and by keeping groups small everyone would encourage each other.

As this was a new concept we really had no idea how it would be received. Lesley double checked with me. 'Are you really sure you can do this Tanya?' I replied 'No problem Lesley, we can do anything. Your readers are going to have some New Sensations'. Our offer was sold out before the magazine went into the shops and extra days were hastily arranged. We live in Kent but people travelled from all over the country, Wales, Scotland, even France – finally we had to call a halt! To round off a very busy 1997 the New Sensations Roadshow went out, the idea behind this was to promote our voice training work and to show some of the work that can be done with any horse or pony.

The feedback from the days and the shows has been tremendous. I have been amazed at the differences in the age groups attending – from very young upwards. We are not promoting something revolutionary but simply the way we as a family have always worked with our horses. The horses should be happy, willing and

wanting to work with us, and most importantly we talk to them. My friends have been badgering me to put our methods into print, so following some serious thinking (not always easy on my part) I felt that if the book offered you our methods and a selection of Sensations to look at, you might be inclined to have a go at some or all of them.

Realistically a dressage training book might have been the obvious choice for me to write but there are plenty of those on the shelf. No, my book has to offer you a very different feel from any others. Personally I cannot get into heavy instructional books which is why each of my lessons is aimed at getting you started and giving you a detailed description but in non-technical language. More importantly to me is that it should appeal to all age ranges with something for everyone. When you pick it up I want it to encourage you to say to yourself 'that looks like fun, I will have a go'. Even if you do not own a horse there are places for lessons or courses. To be honest this has to be one of the most daunting projects that I have taken on, give me a big arena with plenty of people and spotlights anytime!

At a lot of my clinics at home and abroad there seems to be a common denominator. It is surprising how many people get stuck in a rut when working or riding horses. Sometimes tunnel vision sets in rather along the lines of 'I only do dressage', 'I only hack', I only jump', 'I only'. Just as a person who leads a very isolated and narrow lifestyle can develop social problems, so the horse can follow a similar pattern. It can become increasingly bored and stale.

The object of my book is to draw you into a new world of training, breaking down the language barrier and building up your own communication lines. In other words talk to your horse, I do not mean by body language but verbally, build up your own vocabulary of words – it does not matter how old or young you or your equine friends are. It does not matter that they might not have a ballerina's footfall or have the waist of a model. Even the outgrown ponies can have a great quality of life, they do not need to be lawn mowers. Whether you want to compete or not is irrelevant, many of you are involved with horses and ponies for the pleasure and the friendship you get from them so don't forget they also get the same back from you. I hope that by having these Sensations together in one book it will make it easier for you to try them and to get your equine friend working with you, bringing more fun and variety into both of your lives. You can do this work with the horse or pony that you already have and if you are enjoying it so much that you would like to compete then there are some useful addresses at the back of the book.

For those of you who are competition riders or just watch at shows I wonder if you have noticed the same things that I have? Over the years many things have changed within the equestrian scene, some for the good but I am sorry to say some to the detriment of the horse. I feel very strongly that for a lot of riders the horse and pony have become merely vehicles for the rider's success. I am not sure why this is occurring, maybe it is the financial reward for winning classes or selling the horses – prices for good ones are escalating – and even more worrying is that these trainer-riders are also promoting their way of training horses down through the system on to younger riders. According to these riders if a problem arises nine times out of ten the horse is at fault. Today three words can be used to describe some training methods which are seen in the practice ring: 'pressure', 'stress' and 'domination'.

My thoughts are that if a person is happy to work like that in public then how must they work their horses at home? If you ever see someone abusing a horse or pony you must report them to the relevant authorities – it does not matter who they are. I have been shocked to hear what some trainers, even so called 'top' ones, are doing to the horses – what is worse is that the owners and grooms will not say anything for fear of being blacklisted. Do the means justify the end? It is frightening really to think what an animal can be put through in the search for perfection with all the gadgets that have come out to 'help' get the horse into a better outline, on the bit and working more from behind. Another trend at present is that if the horse wants to chew the bit as he is supposed to, then make sure the nose-band is as high as the cheek bones allow and it must be done up as tight as possible! The overall pressure on both the poll and the face must be unbearable. Comfortable and pleasant for the horse, I think not. Put on a riding hat that is too small, then do up the chinstrap as tightly as possible. Your jaw will be clenched, now see if

you can move it. After one hour take off the hat, how does your head feel?

For me it is very important to recognise the fact that not every horse or pony will be able to do the work the owner might have mapped out for him, for either a physical or mental reason. It is important not to try and 'force a round pin into a square hole'. Either you change what you want to do or let your horse move on to someone he will be happy with.

Sometimes, just as we do not get on with every person we meet, so the same situation can arise for people with horses or ponies. I have met people with this problem and their fear is that they are considered failures if they cannot get it together with the horse or pony. If, after a reasonable time of working at trying to get a partnership going, things are not working out then I see nothing wrong in parting company: this way both parties get a better quality of life. It is not admitting defeat but being sensible.

I can only offer you the benefit of my knowledge gained from my parents and quite literally from working all my life with horses of all ages, sizes and characters. I would not be so vain as to say this is the only way to work them, as any trainer will know you can have worked hundreds of horses in your own way but then you will meet one who does not want to know. You come up against a wall and are stuck and you have to start thinking laterally! With every horse you have to get inside his mind to understand him, sometimes a problem is human induced and at other times (but rarely) it is an actual hereditary or physical problem. As the saying goes 'there are many roads to Rome' but I would add to that and say make sure the one you take is the smoothest one, even if it is a bit longer.

Please, before you go galloping off into the sunset do start at the beginning with 'The Start for Life at Any Age'. This I hope gives you an idea about why we work in the manner we do and it will get you thinking and will give both you and your equine friend the chance to enter a new world. By building up trust, confidence and understanding together life becomes much easier. In the case of the young horse, I firmly believe that the more he learns and is handled from the ground before being sat on, not only makes this experience as stress free as possible but also gives him the best start in life. There are four things that I hope will be ingrained in you by the time you have finished this book and they are – talk to your horse, respect each other, have patience and communicate with him.

Are you ready to try a New Sensation or two?

PART 1

THE START FOR LIFE AT ANY AGE

DO YOU SPEAK THE SAME LANGUAGE?

When writing this book I did not include this section and it was only after reading the later chapters that I realised something was missing. I felt I was only giving one part of the picture, and that you really needed the full story to see how we relate to our horses.

As so often happens, when you have been doing something for a very long time you take it for granted and it becomes the norm, you do not even think about what you are doing or saying to the animals. Having to itemise all my thoughts, words and movements on paper, so that you can fully understand and put into practice all that I have written, meant that I needed to go into more detail with the beginning work that we do as standard. I hope that by breaking this into 'compartments' it will make it very clear for you to follow and do.

I have asked 'do you speak the same language?' because it can be very easy to take any animal for granted just because he is always there. Personally I find it interesting to watch and note how people relate to their horse before I talk to them. For some, the horse is simply a means to an end, he is there to do a job and, when the rider has finished, the reins are handed over to the groom. If he is lucky the horse will get a pat on the neck from his rider. By watching the scene and seeing how the horse behaves you can see who he relates to and it will be the one who cares and looks after him. The relationship is between these two and they have their own language and bond.

Over the last few years a lot of books and magazine articles have been written to promote a better understanding of our equine friends. I am not sure that they are all new thoughts, some are ones which were forgotten but, like fashion, have become new again. Often it is just plain common sense that is being written.

I wonder if the lack of understanding of horses has come about over the years quite simply because more people than ever are becoming involved. Unfortunately they often have little or no knowledge of what they are dealing with although that is not to say they will not learn but I feel it may be harder for them as it is not a knowledge that has been handed down.

To speak the same language means to understand your horse so watch him as much as you can, know his moods so that you know what is normal and what is not. Even though the situation might be that you do not groom your horse yourself because of other commitments, please take time to chat (literally) to him in his stable or field even if he has company. For me the important thing is that you are friends, when he sees you he should come over to see you.

On the other hand be careful that you do not let him run your life. I have seen both friendships and partnerships get into serious trouble when the four-legged friends get put over the two-legged variety – everything needs to be kept in perspective!

DO YOU HAVE HIS TRUST?

Trust is not a long word but without it you are on a losing wicket. For both you and your horse any progress will be very limited if indeed possible.

It never ceases to amaze me how horses are expected to work with the rider or handler when they are frightened or confused. When explaining horses' behaviour I liken it to human behaviour. If a person is stressed, tired and is repeatedly made to do something in order to get

In holiday time the minis live together in a big barn overnight, playing out during the day hence Sam's stable stains! Barney, in the distance, is wary of crowds so takes his time but the others come over to see me.

it right, it can be seen that as they get tired, so they do less. Consequently muscle fatigue sets in and he will lose his confidence in his ability to perform.

For the horse it does not matter what age he is, he can lose his trust and confidence at any time of his life if he is worked in such a manner that is not clear to him and this in turn can break him down mentally.

To help him place his trust in you and therefore grow in confidence, it is vitally important everything that is presented for him to learn and understand is done in such a manner that he can cope with it. Patience is a virtue and nothing can replace good calm training which will make the horse grow. He will trust you because you should never give a reason for him to do otherwise. Training, and in this I include

voice training, is best thought of as building blocks with the starting point being the foundations.

It does not matter what type of training you are doing with your horse, without the basics you are more likely to meet problems, even more important is that if you do have a hiccup simply retrace your steps. By doing this you have moved your horse back to the level that he can cope with and it will give you a chance to make sure that you are making your requests clear for your horse to understand what is wanted.

Your horse will show his trust by doing what you ask him to and I do not simply mean the ridden requests. Remember that the horse is a flight animal and it really is amazing what they let us do with them when we put them into what would be considered vulnerable and almost alien situations.

If you look at it in this light I hope that you will really appreciate and maybe understand more why horses can have problems – nearly all are induced by humans who do not really look at things from the horse's point of view. Trust and confidence cannot be earned just by giving lots of titbits, they are gained by a combination of things such as how you handle the horse, your attitude to him, whether you are fair or whether you blow hot and cold – one day all over him, the next shouting if he puts a foot out of place. Finally I suppose you would call it 'horse sense' – that something that is indefinable but which the horse senses in the people who have it. For some it is the most natural gift in the world to be with horses, understanding and reading them, but it is not impossible for others to learn.

Yet taking all this into account you can still come across the 'odd' one. We bred Vinnie who had the same beginnings as all our young stock and was started at the same time as his half-brother Danny. Watching the young colts going around the field one would think that Vinnie was the boss, he would be in the lead and show the way out of the field very confidently. When the time came to prepare for starting the two boys I had quite a surprise at the attitude of the two. Danny was so laid back, not worrying at all as to Vinnie's whereabouts. On the other hand Vinnie was throwing quite a tantrum in his stable, even though there were many other horses close by and he could see them. The panic set in because his security blanket, in this case Danny, had been moved. Whilst Danny was there he was part of Vinnie's routine but when he could not see him he started to worry and get agitated which showed us a basic lack of confidence.

Even though we knew Vinnie's history I must admit I had not foreseen any problems, yet believe it or not his mother has a lot to answer for! Both the boys shared the field with our miniature horses but right from day one the behaviour of their mothers could not have been more different.

From the moment Danny spied the minis in the field his first reaction was to go and play with them but his mother had very different ideas. She went straight after him, pulled him into line and proceeded to take him around the perimeter of the field, once she was happy that he knew the boundaries then he was allowed back to play. Also the behaviour in the stable was interesting to watch. Come feed time, Danny would follow suit by copying his mother who would wait quietly for her feed and would allow him to share her food. There was a lot of interaction between them such as scratching each other all over. Danny was given an excellent start by his mother who taught him trust and gave him confidence, which in turn made our job much easier.

 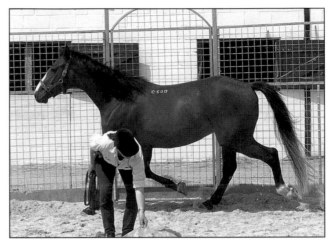

Here is a good comparison between Jack and Vinnie. They are the same age, have had the same handling but their attitude to the plastic shows you much, proving the point that every horse is an individual. Jack is very laid back and inquisitive, whereas Vinnie is highly strung and wary of new things. Interestingly, Vinnie had no worries when it came to loading into the horse box. I let him sniff the ramp and he followed me straight up, showing his trust and confidence in me.

Vinnie on the other hand had a mother who I can only say belted him whenever he stepped out of line. Just after the birth she looked superb and her condition had not dropped off at all. The reason was very simple, the meat she had kept on should have gone through the system to Vinnie, who popped out looking like a bag of bones! I am sorry to say she was a very selfish mother from the start. In the stable when he had finished eating he would move over to her manger but she would not share and her ears went back and she would kick out. It did not matter if Vinnie was in the way, as he often was in the beginning. We found out at a later date that as a youngster she had a very bad beginning, never getting enough food and her mother had little or no milk.

On their first field outing all his mother wanted to do was eat the grass and her attitude to Vinnie showed in his behaviour with the other horses, whereas Danny was forward and inquisitive to meet the others. Vinnie's treatment during the few days before they were intermingled with the group had a very obvious effect on him. He held back unsure of the reaction and reception he would receive from the other horses. Over a period of time he did mix but on the whole he clung to Danny.

His start in life has affected him and his attitude, and when working with him, if something is done differently he gets upset. When handling a character as complex as this, it is one step forward and two back at times. He cannot be rushed but one really has to understand the horse's mind and behaviour. Sometimes it is lack of confidence which causes an upset or then he might use that as an excuse. It is therefore imperative for Vinnie that he learns that changes do happen and he need not be afraid. For instance the first time that he was tied up in the grooming room where he could not see any other horses he threw what I would call a paddy

Idolo and Illustre out for a morning spin with me and Louise.

or tantrum and was whinnying his head off. He was not wanting to stand still and quietly eat his hay but was moving around sideways, getting hot and agitated.

Anyway, I carried on with my work and left him with the radio playing soft music – I didn't think he needed heavy rock to add to his brain waves! He was only left for a short time to start with, I could hear him all the time and he could hear us next door to him. Then I would pop in and make a big fuss giving him a carrot, after doing this a couple of times I then put him back into his stable.

Over a period of days I built up the time he was on his own and after about four days he was very relaxed and happy to wait in his box. He knew that he would get a reward for it and he was gaining in confidence. It was very important not to go in and stand with him all the time he was creating and if I had done he would have been rewarded for doing something that I did not want him to do.

So it is important to have time and patience in abundance and be prepared to work quietly through the problems, obviously making any alterations necessary to the training programme.

Every horse is different and to enable him to have the best future possible it is important to listen to him. For Vinnie's future we will partner him with a special person with whom he can bond and so carry on progressing with life.

DO YOU RESPECT EACH OTHER?

I debated whether or not to put this under a separate heading or to tie it in with the previous one. Whilst they are fairly close, I feel that is is possible to have your horse's trust but not his respect.

In my dictionary one of the terms given to cover respect is 'to show consideration'. For me respect is a two-way conversation between the rider/handler and the horse. It really does not matter what you do with him, he may be 'only' a hack, a riding school horse or even a competition horse, but he deserves consideration. It all boils down to the same thing – every being is entitled to respect.

I was invited to give a display and talk to promote our voice training work at a specialist gala day. For the itinerary a name was required for our training system, and after much thought I came up with 'The Larrigan T.E.C.H.' meaning the Training of Equines Compassionately and Humanely. I was later questioned quite strongly as to why I had used those words and, as is my way, I said exactly what I thought. From my experience of seeing horses and ponies in many situations, not only at competitions and not only in this country, the regard for animals has gone downhill. There appears to be a lack of respect for them. I do not mean everybody behaves in this manner but more cases are being reported.

There is simply no possible reason why an animal is not given enough food or water to live and we all know that without these basic necessities it cannot survive. I cannot begin to describe some of the atrocities that we have been called out to assist with and what is so shameful is that it does take a period of time for any animal to go beyond the point of no return. The lack of respect for life is not just with the person(s) who committed the offence but with those others who saw but either said nothing or said that 'they did not see'. After all when we see a person who is anorexic we do not have to be doctors to know that something is not right.

The above is for me a very obvious lack of respect. However, when you see a horse who looks to be in good condition, has a shiny coat and well cared for feet, and is competing at the highest level, would you ever believe that he is mentally abused? You might wonder how it is that a horse can be mentally abused but obviously does not show the same symptoms as a human. For some, one only has to look at him, often he will not want the person who schools or trains him to be near, yet that does not mean that he will not let them ride him. Often horses are too generous for their own good, they keep on giving but the rider wants more and more, always searching for perfection. If the horse makes a mistake, however small, he is reprimanded and consequently he starts to anticipate the punishment. Eventually the horse cannot cope with the pressure. He will show it possibly by getting tense and very agitated, sweating profusely, making more mistakes then getting into a bigger panic about it or he can, as we say, 'switch off' becoming stale in his work and not enjoying it, looking like a zombie. This relates not only to working on the flat but with other equestrian activities.

We have had many horses sent to us for re-

starting including some from abroad and one of these was a really interesting case. A mare working at Grand Prix dressage level had gone to a yard sale for sale but she was very tense and wary, especially when ridden by men. My friend asked me to fly over and have a look at her. Before doing anything with her my priority was to get to know her and see her in the stable. The staff warned me to 'watch' her but I went in loaded with goodies – I find that, used in the right way, food can be a great help when trying to make friends with a worried horse. It is of the upmost importance that you respect a horse's space, particularly if he is worried. I went inside the stable and stayed by the door. All the time I kept talking to her and waited for her to come to me, at which she was most surprised. When she heard the rustle of the Polo-mint wrapper she stretched out her neck but did not move her feet; the first thing I noticed was she had the most lovely eyes, big and dark brown. Eventually the rest of her body followed and all of the goodies were consumed! Whilst my coat was given a thorough investigation for more Polos I took the opportunity to give her neck a good scratch then I moved up to her head.

I am not the sort to generalise but she was not the type of horse that you would expect to behave in this wary and tense manner. To cut a long story short, I rode her over a period of three days. Her attitude spoke volumes; if you moved an inch she was petrified and started offering every movement she thought you wanted. Luckily for her my friend decided to send her over to us so that she could get her confidence in humans back and start living again. It took a while but time, our situation and the work we did gave her back a life. There would, however, always be the slight unsureness of new men, although from day one she adored my father

who chatted to her every night and on seeing him she would start calling for her carrots. One can only wonder just what she had gone through, for her the lack of respect she had been shown was frightening.

It is interesting and worrying at the same time to note that the F.E.I., to which all the international shows are affiliated, has over the past few years brought in a code of conduct as to how horses should be treated. We have to ask what is happening to the trainers and riders; is it just a few who require this code?

One must applaud the equestrian federations which are now making a stand for horses' rights. At present I believe Germany is leading the way with cameras and much stronger stewarding at its shows and is even visiting trainers' yards.

It might seem that I am going on rather about the lack of respect that seems to be shown towards horses but to me it appears that this side of horsemanship is sadly lacking and not being passed down. There is one activity that really does nothing for me and that is what we call gymkhanas. It is said that they build team spirit but from what I have seen and heard, one wonders. Most of the time riders are too big for the ponies and speed is of the essence, style has no meaning, and the ponies are seemingly pulled from pillar to post. I must admit I did try it once but never again, even if my pony had let me pick up the red flags!

As I have said, this is only my opinion but I do wonder what exactly is being taught. I am pleased though to see that people in Britain are at last realising the benefit of vaulting. This is a discipline which I promote in my Roadshows and is something that I learnt in my youth as a matter of course in the circus and it has been practised on the continent for many years. For those of you who have not seen vaulting, the

Vaulting is now becoming a recognised sport in this country.

vaulter rides the horse bareback (although in competition work the horses do have a pad on their backs) and performs a series of exercises including standing up on his quarters whilst the horse is cantering. The horse is controlled by a handler on a lunge line and works on a circle in a very collected canter. He wears a bridle, side-reins and a roller. The roller has special hand grips which give you great assistance when mounting, as you must canter in rhythm next to the horse holding the grips and then swing yourself up onto his back. It sounds so easy but it does take practice! Vaulting is brilliant for the rider's balance, posture and feel and I believe it teaches respect, trust, confidence and how to read the horse.

Remember respect is all about taking responsibility for the horse that is in your care, never wanting more than he can give you, acknowledging his strengths, weaknesses and working together as a partnership. Fear does not equate to respect.

So what about the horse, how does he handle the respect aspect of his life, how does he show it? If you have not seen horses interacting together it would be in your interest to go and watch them; the eldest is not always in charge. For me the funniest sights have to be when the minis are out with the big ones. Sparky our yearling colt who is all of twenty-nine inches (74cm) tall is at the moment learning his place in the herd but does not always accept it. He tries to show his authority by standing on the bank in the field and then proceeds to have a boxing match with anyone who comes near his territory. The other minis just ignore him as the troublesome upstart but the big old boy Embassy will play with him for so long, then when the pinch nipping gets too much he will remind Sparky who is the boss by gently pushing him off his high perch! All the horses out in the fields have respect for each other and have pecking orders, so that when a bale of hay is put out for them to eat, the one closest to it will come straight away but will give way to the one who is over them.

Horses know their own minds and have amazing memories. I believe they can read people – they can sense and smell our moods and fears. From the way we talk to them, handle them and our attitude, all these signs give the horse signals as to the manner in which he will respond. They will help him to know if he can trust and respect us or whether he can push the boundaries back and effectively take charge, in other words show a total lack of respect.

For those of you who have just come into horses or only have a limited access to them, this might sound rather a strange statement. But look at it this way, to see a small person either leading or riding a large horse whilst at the same time being in control and at one with their horse can be surprising. This is because for some, size and

strength are tied misleadingly together to equate control. The mutual respect of horse and rider/handler allows them to work together – take a look at the small flat-racing jockey who is able to control the muscle and power of the racehorse. The properly prepared and well-trained horse will have respect for his rider who also has a considerable technique, which is not strength. A racehorse that is frightened is quite simply a danger to himself, the jockey and the other horses.

On one of my clinics abroad I worked with two amazing riders and their horses. One rider had been disabled through an accident and the other lady had been a Thalidomide baby and had deformed arms. Yet to watch these two women at work would put many to shame – they did everything for their horses. Equally so, watching the horses assist their owners with the tacking up, by lowering their heads and standing stock still while being mounted also made one realise just what horses can do for people, physically and mentally. Both said that their horses helped them and that they could sense the moods the girls were in. For me it shows very strongly the bonds that are formed and without the trust and respect of either party it would have been a non-starter.

As I have said elsewhere no two horses are the same, it is possible for people to have a good understanding and working partnership with their own horse but that does not mean to say that they will get that same respect from other horses, much depends on the horse's character, upbringing and training as well as their own actual ability. I think it is important for people to acknowledge this fact. Serious problems can arise when people overestimate their ability, they do not recognise this but the horse does. A classic example is when a horse changes hands. For a period of time everything goes well but eventually problems set in, often with jumping or with the young horse napping, when they start to realise that the rider/handler is unsure, not confident, possibly even frightened. As a result the horse 'tests' them by pushing a little bit further, finding eventually that the ground rules have been moved, thereby letting him take control. Believe it or not this can in fact frighten the horse and so a vicious circle is formed, if this arises help must be sought before someone is injured or a good horse ruined.

A common problem we have met is that of the horse barging out of the stable as the door is being opened. Obviously this is highly dangerous. This sort of behaviour does not do the horse any good at all, let alone the person on the floor. Barging often starts with the horse standing at the door anticipating either going out or being turned out in the field, the problem is that he has not learnt to go back and wait before the person steps inside the stable. I always ask my horses to move back before I go in and I do not walk them straight out the minute the door is opened – they must wait. Forming correct and safe habits in the beginning makes it much easier for the horse and rider.

To round off this section I would say that if you are thinking of changing horses for whatever reason or maybe getting your first horse it really is worthwhile making sure you are one hundred per cent honest with yourself about your ability. Not only do you need to be fair to yourself but also to the horse. Ambition is good and necessary if you aim to make it but not if you are setting unrealistic goals for yourself and your horse because (a) you will never make it and (b) you will never be happy, and then you could become one of those people who always blames

their horse. Remember you will only get as good as you give and to get respect you must give it to earn it.

WHAT DO YOU WANT FROM HIM?

I feel this section is relevant because it is very easy to go and buy a horse or pony. I often wonder if enough thought goes into what is really going to be required from the horse in the first place. Often in the case of ponies they are presents from non-horsey parents. The ponies are much adored for a period of time, then the novelty wears off and the dark rainy nights set in, excuses are given as to why this and that cannot be done, so in time he becomes neglected but mum and dad will make sure some food is thrown his way.

I only wish that before anyone got a horse or pony they helped out at a stables in all weathers for some time so that they fully understood what they were undertaking with the new responsibility.

It saddens me to hear people say 'my horse cannot do this' or 'it cannot do that' or 'it is no good'. Nine times out of ten it is not the horse that has a problem but the rider who is making communication errors, so it stands to reason the poor animal is going to be totally confused and it might even get to the point when he will not respond to any question.

The other scenario is that whilst in the beginning the horse was fine for the job for which it was intended, over a period of time the owner's requirements have changed. Very possibly they are looking towards higher competition and whereas the horse was able to cope with the lower level the next stage might

well be beyond him. Then his owner must sit back and give serious thought as to whether or not their horse can progress or can they cope with their horse's limitations. Too often one sees horses which are being what we call 'overfaced' or 'overstretched', I do not mean only by trying to jump fences that are too big for them but also doing work that is physically or mentally difficult. By not acknowledging that their horse is getting into trouble, they then conclude he is being difficult and not wanting to try. This in turn can only make life very uncomfortable for the horse and possibly frustrating for the owner. I would consider this serious crunch time. Everything is relevant and sometimes one needs to accept the horse's limitation and make the best of it.

Many moons ago, when I was about ten years old, my parents gave me a smashing pony called Cobber. Do not get me wrong, because I said 'smashing' it does not mean that he was the best money could buy. He was the best our money could buy. My parents always worked very hard to build up our horse business and create a living for us and one of the ways they did this was to buy horses with problems, re-educate them and sell them on. So when they met Cobber they felt he would carry me for a few years. However there was one 'if' with him, that being that he did not really like to jump coloured fences! In other words you could not guarantee getting around a course of jumps but Mum and Dad reckoned I would learn from him! I owe him a debt of gratitude because I certainly learned how to sit a sticky jumper – he had the most amazing technique.

It did not matter at what speed we approached a fence – he only had short choppy strides and he could not stand off a fence – he would always put in a 'short one' in other words canter, canter

All equines enjoy mutual grooming and Cinderella and Tom Tom are no exception. If your horse is on his own, the grooming and attention you give him are more important than just keeping him clean.

stop and jump, sometimes like a cat, all four feet leaving the ground at the same time! The combinations were always exciting as were the the spread fences. My parents would close their eyes but I had total faith that he would never let me down. I always dreamt of competing at the All England Show Jumping Ground at Hickstead – it was and still is the mecca. Anyway I sent off my entries for the four-day show and felt very confident, though when Dad and I walked the course I did think they were a little on the large side. Poor Cobber must have thought he had died but not gone to heaven, he took one look at those fences and I got as far as the first one!

Anyway, not only had he taught me to stick his awkward jumping but he had also taught me to have faith and perseverance. Dad would phone home and say 'well, we got a bit further

around the course today'. By day four the ground was in our favour. Following all-night rain, it did not suit the other ponies who were slipping and sliding everywhere. Fortunately for us the course builder had left the course the same as the day before. Cobber was in his element, his short strides just right for the going. I must admit it was not the most elegant of rounds but we went clear earning a rosette and prize money. I was so proud of that Hickstead cheque I never cashed it, that way I could look at it. My parents said it would have been cheaper to have bought a cheque but at least Cobber and I achieved my dream. It did not matter that he was never going to be Showjumper of the Year! To me he was simply the best. He never left me until the day he was buried when he was well into his twenties.

Miniature horses are also becoming more popular but often their new owners do not totally realise that they need the same treatment as their larger counterparts and it is just as important for them to have regular checks for worms, teeth and feet. They do rather tend to be used as mobile lawn mowers or just pets, yet both the miniatures and their owners can get so much more out of life by aiming to incorporate most of the work described in this book.

During our Roadshow tours I deliberately show how the miniature horses or small ponies can do more work than they are often asked for. Many of the comments passed referred to the training we did with them, often people said that they had quite simply not thought about it. I have often heard parents saying that the rider is at school so the pony doesn't get worked in winter time. I don't see why the parents cannot learn to do this work. That way the pony is still kept stimulated and in some form of work, so when the weekend comes around it does not get

a nasty shock, especially if it is an older pony. Even a show pony enjoys a change – variety is the spice of life – and it can be protected with bandages so there is no chance of it blemishing itself.

In the USA miniatures get the full treatment with their shows, having very full programmes and a big following. This is now spreading through the UK and Europe but remember you do not need shows to give your little ones a life.

There is a trend that I worry about and that is people buying stallions. It does not matter what breed it is or whether it is a well-behaved horse, unless the horse is going to be used for breeding then he is about to engage in a life that will be devoid of another horse's contact. I am not anti stallions and we have five in our mixed yard at the moment. They are treated in the same way as the rest of our equines. Our mini stallions run with the geldings because they were inter-mingled at a young age, the big stallions who are here for training, are lovely and well-mannered, they run out in their paddocks and can see the other horses across the avenues. They are no trouble but it is sad they cannot have a chin-wag and a scratch with another horse.

If you either keep or are going to keep one horse on his own, think very carefully about the life you are going to give him. It is well documented that the horse is a herd creature, so much thought should be given to how it will be kept mentally and physically stimulated. Mind you, even those of ours who go out with their mates and have regular grooming like nothing more than a good scratch in their more inaccessible regions! There are now more playthings coming on the market for horses to help keep them occupied, but with a little ingenuity you can make some pretty interesting items.

From the riding side do try to ride out with others if you can, not only for the obvious safety reasons but if you wish to compete then it is good for your horse to socialise otherwise life could be rather exciting when he gets amongst other horses. Even if it is only hacking out, do not forget they do make friends.

Whilst it might not be possible for you to have another equine do think maybe about another animal which can act as a companion. We have five cats (rescued and neutered, we do not need any help expanding our animal population!) along with dogs, mini goats, ducks and geese. No, these are not as companions to our horses but more rescue cases! Anyway, getting back on track, it is very interesting to see the cats playing with the horses on the door of their stables although rather risky with the stallions. So far all the cats still have ears and tails intact!

I read about a very famous racehorse who had high hopes resting on him but at the races he would be depressed and off his feed. Luckily his trainer was on the ball and realised he was missing his friend the sheep. Thereafter the sheep accompanied him everywhere with his own pass and much success!

Finally, how about this for a change of direction? A friend of mine, Jan, has my retired international horse Diplomat. Over the last few years she has had great fun learning the more advanced work with him but he is now twenty-two and feeling his joints a bit and is having to cut back on the big trots and canters he used to do. He has been given a new lease of life in a new direction teaching Jan's husband Western riding. He loves the sedate jogs and lopes as well as the trail sections. Who says you cannot teach an old dog new tricks!

WHAT DOES HE NEED FROM YOU?

This seems a fairly reasonable question does it not? How would you answer it? I asked a couple of friends who basically gave the same reply: a warm stable, food, water, shoeing, routine, care and attention, the vet when sick and not to be taken advantage of or roughed up.

All the above are right but I would like it to be taken further and I would like to explain exactly what I mean by the phrase 'The Start for Life at Any Age'.

I feel that the more that is introduced to your horse as soon as you are able, in turn helps to get you both on the same wavelength. For me there is so much you can do with your horse and I do not mean in the sense of competitions but even competition horses need a change sometimes.

It is so easy to get into a habit of doing things the same way but, if you sit down and really think about it, are you and your horse getting as much as possible from the partnership? No, I know you cannot take him out to a candlelight dinner although I remember making my pony a special carrot cake for his birthday! But life can become boring and stale for your horse if it is the same day in day out, even if he is given the necessities. On the other side some people never let a horse be a horse – remember he likes to have a buck, a roll, get dirty, it's normal, but preferably not when I am riding them. So I make sure all our horses, little and large, have play time in some form or other. It is not really fair on the horse to put him in an unnatural situation where he is never allowed to express himself, he needs freedom in some manner or form. Particularly for the young horse whose fun may not be yours. By showing the older horse

(Right) Idolo loves his free runs so he can really express himself!

different things, stretching his brain, working his body and consequently loosening his joints you can bring another dimension into your lives.

Before I progress any further, and without sounding condescending, I would like to say that if you are thinking of getting an unmade or newly started horse, if you have never assisted, started or worked with a very green one before, please think very carefully. It does take experience and knowledge to be able to do it properly and safely for both you and the horse. If you do, then it is worthwhile having a knowledgeable person give you the once over every now and then, just to check you are going in the right direction.

I have met people who have bought unridden youngsters at six years old. I must add that they ran into fairly serious trouble when trying to start the horses off at this age. There can be genuine reasons as to why the horse has been left so long but equally so you will not always be given the truth. It is possible that the horse was started when younger but there were problems, so the trainer backed off to give the horse a break. If the original trainer neglects to tell the prospective purchaser the full history, one can imagine the problems which are about to be encountered.

Over the last few years there have been books, videos and lecture demonstrations all promoting how quickly you can ride an unmade horse if you do it in a certain manner. Much is made of the theory that if you send him away and ignore him then he will come to you, all depending on how you present yourself to the horse. If the ideas and actions promoted help people to understand the workings of the horse's mind and the reasons why he does something then that is good but what also has to be remembered is that the horse is a living being

with his own mind. I feel so much depends on the horse's breed, his mental attitude, age and previous handling: what works with one might not work on another.

Personally, I worry that people believe that by buying the book and video they think that they are in a position to start off young horses. One might read about the different signals that the horse and trainer give to each other, but reflexes and the ability to read the horse does on the whole take time to develop. Some people never do develop them and it is not for the want of trying. There are others who relate to the horse in such a manner that is not taught but is born in them – they are the privileged few. For all that is being promoted I will always say that the more the young horse learns from you on the floor and as early as possible then the easier the next step forward will be and in my opinion the safer for both. He will have trust and confidence in you as his trainer and friend because he knows his words, he has a good mouth and his muscles are ready to carry a rider.

You need to know your horse, his moods, likes and dislikes. If you find there is a change in character, you must analyse the run-up to it. Possibly it is pain and discomfort from something he has done to himself in the stable. The tack might not fit correctly, teeth might need doing or in a mare there might be problems with her ovaries. It might be that a change in feed is required. Not only are there so many different types of feed stuffs now available but there are analysts who can help point you in the right direction.

It is important that you use your eyes and hands so that you know his body and where all the lumps and bumps are that are normal for him. This is particularly true of the legs especially down the tendon area. Just grooming

him is not really enough.

Often people give their horse's head and ears a good rub but do not go any further. If you have not done it before try giving your horse a massage. I think this is particularly important if your horse is on his own, basically you will take the place of another horse giving him a good scratch! It is rewarding to see how relaxed he becomes and one of the main areas where I find horses need work is the neck. When I am giving lessons to riders with their horses, I always give the horse the once over to check that there are not any tension knots. If there are they will obviously cause a problem, so I will show how to ease them by just rubbing with the fingers and asking the horse to stretch his neck round and down.

I also tend to work around and inside the mouth, all the time talking to him. I ease my fingers inside and under his lips and rub his gums. You do need to be alert while doing this exercise! This can help with dentistry work and when you worm he will take the applicator into his mouth more easily.

An interesting exercise is to see if you are able to put your horse's bridle or headcollar on from a low position. If you can do this then you are seeing just how much trust and confidence he has in you because he is putting himself into a very vulnerable position.

All our horses lift their legs when asked verbally and with pressure from the thumb on the side of the leg. I bend the legs and slowly stretch them forward then bring them back and put them down. This is very good for the muscles and, for the youngster, this work is of the utmost value in preparing him for the farrier.

Anything that you do to your horse which will prepare him for the trials and tribulations that he may meet in life can only be for the good, for instance I will stand by the tractor and talk to the driver. I have often heard people say 'be quiet, don't make a noise' 'watch this or that', this type of handling can make a horse wary and he ends up anticipating and wondering what is about to happen. Walk him over plastic, pass bright objects, drag noisy things around, but remember when you begin just use small pieces otherwise he might get a fright. He should be able to tie up and wait for you, as well as standing untied when asked. You will see how we go about this in a later chapter and also you may note that some of the exercises we do are not always done as the norm, such as leaving plastic bags in the stable, hanging things in front of the doorway and some of the groundwork, but they can help the horse at any age. The right handling can set the horse up for life. We are also lucky with some of our extras, such as the walker, which all the horses go on, and the electric groomer. This not only stimulates the muscles but gets the horses used to noises and consequently clipping. Our machine is great and is still going strong after twenty-five years – it has certainly seen a few horses!

In this book I am not taking you from the start of a horse's life but am assuming that he has been started. I do, however, think that you will find much of our work is relevant to any age.

There is one final thing that your horse might well need from you and it is possible that you cannot bear to think of making the decision to call the vet. But we do owe it to our horses to look after them at the end of their time and not to pass them on. On speaking to my vet about this she told me that at the market she had seen either old horses who at one time had been good at their job or those who had a problem that was going to get worse and their owners could not face it.

We are both of the opinion that it is the quality of life that is of the utmost importance to any animal and it is not fair on them to try and stretch time out whilst they go downhill. Our feelings have to be put on the side and we must do what is right for them. I do not consider it to be playing 'God' to make the decision, but the fact is we have taken the horse out of the wild, thereby removing him from his predators who would be there if he was ill. One of the hardest ones I had to let go was my pony Swop, I had grown up with her and she was fantastic. Perhaps she was not fantastic in the accepted sense but, to me, in her thirties she looked amazing with a good body on her and no one realised how old she was. Unfortunately she developed a bad breathing problem, and her flanks would give a double heave to get her breath. When she breathed out you could hear the wheeze due to the lungs struggling. We gave her the medications and they helped a little but I was not happy. One night I decided that I was going to sit with her as it was hot, humid and the air was still. It was ten times worse for her at night, which I had not realised and particularly if she was lying down. I heard her struggling for air and the next day I let her go. Unfortunately this type of problem is becoming more common with horses of all ages, whether it is due to all the pesticides that have been used I do not know.

Another scenario which is hard to deal with is to have an old horse who does not have an obvious problem but who is losing weight. Normally this is because the teeth, which do eventually wear down or drop out, can no longer grind the food and the digestive system starts to fail and basically he is starving to death. It is neither right nor fair to the horse to let him suffer, even though a heartbreaking decision has to be made. These two examples that I have mentioned appear, from speaking to my vet, to be the most common problems that owners have to cope with. I have always made the decision for my horses, yet when speaking to 'amateur' owners I have been surprised at the lack of help and advice they have had from their vets when the end is inevitable but is being delayed. I am sorry but I do not think it is right that an animal's life is prolonged by the vet to spare our feelings and for me the vet's priority is to the animal.

CAN YOUR HORSE BEND, WILL HE MOVE AWAY FROM PRESSURE?

I am very fortunate and happy to be able to work with riders of all levels and often they just want to improve their horses. One of the most common problems I come across is that horses do not bend easily because they are very stiff laterally through their sides and neck and also over the top from the quarters up over the back. The other common problem is that they do not move off or away from the leg.

Sometimes it goes hand in hand that a horse which does not respond to the leg is also dead in the mouth although this is not always the case. I do not work on the philosophy that every rider can ride their horse through the problem, thereby getting the back end working which in turn lightens the front end and hey presto you are then able to work him down and round to stretch him and bring him up again.

If there is a problem I will ask the rider to go to halt and this gives both of them time to think about what I am asking them to do. By re-establishing themselves at the halt, the rider then talks down the rein to the horse's mouth by opening and closing their fingers, asking him to

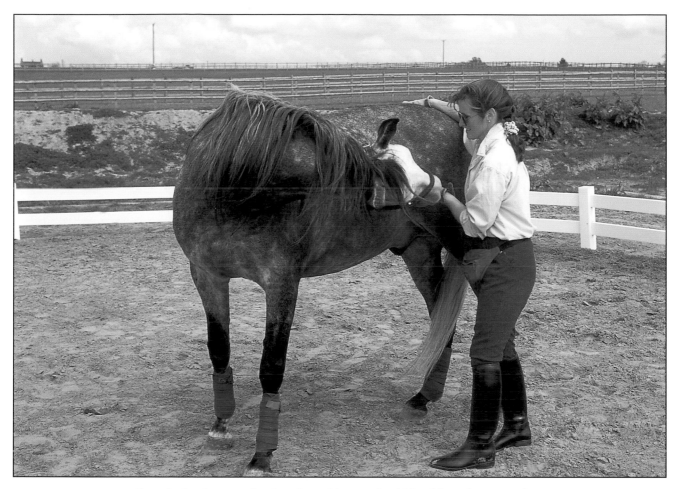

Once he has learnt to bend in the stable you should be able to do it anywhere.

relax his jaw and give to the rein when asked. This work and the progress on from it is covered in greater detail in the Western section.

As I have said earlier, the more your horse learns from the ground the easier the next stage will be, this also includes lateral work. If your horse has learnt to move from your aid, which is the hand replacing the leg, and has also learnt the verbal aids, then when ridden or long reined he already knows what the words mean. This makes life much easier for both of you.

Starting at the very beginning in the stable you can teach your horse his 'ABC'. I like the horses to be tied up when they are in the stables, this is not because I do not trust them but safety is the most important aspect when working with horses for both human and animal. If, as in our case, people are working and learning the trade with you, the law on safety is very strong. It does not matter how quiet and docile the horse is but a fork and a loose horse in the stable can be a lethal combination.

When doing your horse in the stable analyse what you do. For instance is it just a case of push him over or let him walk around? If you do either of these then try keeping one hand on the headcollar, place your other hand just behind the girth area and with your fingers or thumb gently get him to move away from the pressure, at the same time you need to give a verbal aid 'side' or 'over'. He will connect the movement to the word as long as you always do the two simultaneously. Obviously he will not be sure what is wanted in the beginning, so you need to make it as clear as possible. Keeping the horse's head to the wall stops the forward momentum and in order to move from your persuading fingers he will step sideways through the only escape route. In doing this movement and by keeping his shoulders still and turning his quarters around he is learning the beginnings of turn on the forehand. Any response, however little, from your horse must be rewarded with verbal praise.

There are some other exercises you can do which will help your horse with any stiffness. Stand your horse by the wall and ask him to stretch his neck around to you. In the beginning you have to be very careful that you do not ask for too much bend or he will just bring the shoulders round, by keeping next to the wall he cannot swing his quarters out. It is important that you make it as clear as possible what you want your horse to do, give him a word for what you are asking him to do. Be satisfied with little and reward with plenty of pats and 'good boys' – verbal encouragement and the ever-helpful carrot, can work tremendously. Before you do anything always check that you know exactly what you are wanting your horse to give you.

As with all work you do with your horse it is important that your exercises are done from both sides.

Another very good exercise is the stretch, which I am sure you have seen your horse do, often after he gets up. You will be shown how to train this in the Voice Training section.

However if your horse does stretch in his stable really study him, note at what point he does it – is it in the same place? By all accounts you should be able to get him to associate your verbal aid with the stretch. You might need to just touch him on the girth area as well. It is important that he is confident with you standing next to him at the same time as he stretches and after a period of time he will put the two together and do it on request. This is a very good exercise for the shoulders and back.

The horse will move from pressure not only sideways but backwards. Again we start by keeping the horse close to the wall and nose up to the wall. With one hand on his chest and the other gently on his side, to prevent him swinging his quarters away from the wall, I tap his chest with my fingers and tell him 'back' and because of the positioning the only way he can go is back. The slightest backward response from him must be rewarded immediately. You can also hold the headcollar and apply the pressure with your hand on the rope and the minute he responds ease off the pressure then praise him. Again do not forget the verbal aid.

HOW MANY NATURAL AND ARTIFICIAL AIDS DO YOU USE?

I have included this short section because over the last few years there seem to be many new products or gadgets coming on the market that

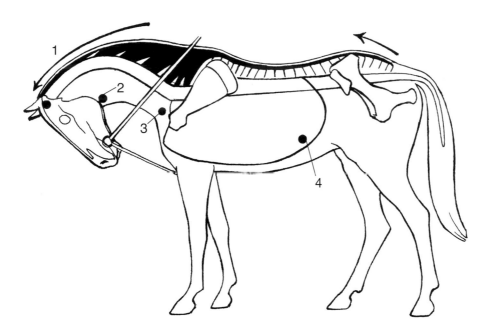

The position seen here is not even an extreme case of being worked badly in draw reins but the problems are still the same:
1 The ligament running from the poll to pelvis will be overstretched
2 Pulling on the base of the skull
3 Tension at the base of the neck
4 The diaphragm will be tightened up

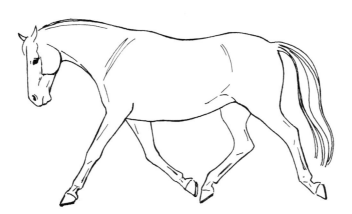

See the difference here in the outline of the horse working without 'help'.

will 'help' the rider get the horse into a better outline.

Look around you when you are next out and about, check out and see how many of the riders are using only the natural aids which consist of voice, legs, seat and the back.

The artificial aids are whips, spurs and martingales but I feel that one can really add to that list because the amount of extras that are coming on to the market is almost worrying. Occasionally there is a place for some of these things in the hands of experts as a re-schooling aid. I can only say I am always amazed that people really do not know the damage that can be caused when a horse is schooled badly with gadgets on. Often one cannot see what is happening but, inside, muscular and even skeletal problems can occur. I spoke to a physiotherapist who had treated horses worked in such a manner and she said it was heartbreaking to see some of the horses she worked on simply being put straight back into draw reins and worked with their heads between their knees. I was surprised to see in a book written by a rider that their horses go into draw reins as a matter of course from day one. I worry that younger riders will follow the same route.

Just a short mention about whips. It seems to be more common for people to use schooling whips. On the minus side it needs to be remembered that these whips can do a lot of damage if used incorrectly, not only will they mark the horse but due to the stinging action they can set up more of a resistance when used too strongly.

I have met some people who, if you mention dressage to them, turn pale! Really it is just training, no matter what you want to do, and your horse should be light in the hand, responsive and as supple as you can make him. Look at a person who never does any type of exercise, they normally have some problems later in life and it is the same for a horse.

I'm sure that one should not need a lot of extra assistance if horses are worked in the correct manner, given time to learn and allowed to digest what is being asked. As I said earlier, there are many roads to Rome. In other words try to pick the road that gives the smoothest ride even if it takes a little longer.

PART 2

GET STARTED WITH LIBERTY AND VOICE TRAINING

INTRODUCTION

The first time I presented this work at a lecture demonstration a person was overheard to say in a derogatory fashion 'this is circus'. To me this is a very insular attitude. Often those who pass such remarks have no real understanding of the horse nor do they have any appreciation of the horse's learning ability or of the trainer who is working with the horse. Some of the top trainers in the world have been involved with the circus, however there are some points to remember when comparing classical high school to competition dressage. Due to the size of the working area the horses most suited to high school work are compact with short, active strides, and lend themselves to the collected work required. A big horse with a lot of movement would, over a period of time, incur much stress on his joints. For me as a rider and trainer of both types of work it is essential that he is ridden classically and presented correctly, sadly this is not always so.

Another word that is used to define the work is 'tricks' as in the Spanish Walk, the stretch and sitting down. If you watch horses at play or even when they get up from lying down and when they stay in the sitting position for a while, you will see them doing a shortened version of one of the above 'tricks'. I use the word 'movement' for the majority of the work you will see in this section. You will also see that I have include some 'tricks', for me this means the horse doing something that he would not normally do but he learns to do when requested by you. For instance holding something for me, pushing me over, even pulling off his blanket.

For the movements I am simply increasing and lengthening the amount of work my horse already does, training him to respond when I ask so that in time he will do the movement whenever I give him the aid no matter where we are. Instead of him only lifting one leg up to strike out at another horse or an irritating fly we ask him to walk forward and keep lifting his legs one after the other. This becomes the Spanish Walk and, as with any work that is done correctly, can be beneficial to the horse. For those who insist on calling all the work 'tricks' then I feel they must include many of the advanced dressage movements under that category.

Sometimes a horse will offer you something completely different that he had never been trained to do. This has happened to me a few times. For instance when Laddie was learning the stretch, he suddenly started crossing his front legs as he went down and putting his head to one side. As I thought it looked rather good I decided to give him a word and reward for doing

this movement. Also by giving him a word and plenty of praise for what he was offering me I put him onto the verbal aid. By doing this I can also say 'no' if he offered it when I didn't ask.

Liberty work is the forgotten side of horse training and for me is quite simply the most fascinating. The interpretation of the word 'liberty' can offer different meanings from being free in the field doing what he wants, to working at liberty in an arena without a rider but following the cues from the trainer.

For those of you who have been to the circus, no doubt you will have seen anything up to twenty stallions in the ring together, all working in complete control, harmony and understanding with their trainer. Sometimes the horses will work with no harness, which obviously makes it harder. It is not just a case of going round the ring but the horses are trained to work through a series of exercises which all form part of the routine. It is very important to remember that without trust and respect you will get nothing from any horse. In return the trainer must have total confidence that his horse(s) will work when asked. In some instances the horse(s) will have hacked out for exercise in the morning but they may have to go in for their show without any warm up, as there is no space available or the weather is poor.

Do not mistake the term 'loose schooling' for liberty work. This is another form of working the horse free, but is different in as much as the arena is larger and normally two people will send the horse around either just to exercise him or send him over jumps.

Jack shows his response when I ask him to halt from canter. Note in the middle photograph how he engages his hind legs underneath his body and so settles in what will be a square halt.

Idolo and me after finishing work for a photographic shoot on Voice Training.

In liberty work forget everything that has been said about the aids, because in this section you will basically only use one aid. This is a 'natural' one and is the voice. You will also require a lunge whip, purely as an extension of your arm, and it is there only to assist you in the beginning because you will get to a point where you can work your horse only by your voice and body movements however slight.

No doubt some of you may well wonder why you should bother with this type of work with your horse. For me this side of working with horses brings training and the understanding of the horse's mind and memory into a new dimension. It enables you to get on a wavelength with a horse that means both of you work in such a manner that after a period of time you feel you are reading each other's minds. There is no contact in the accepted sense of the word as with riding or long reining so the onus is purely on you and your ability to express your wishes to your horse in a manner he can understand and translate into a movement. It is very difficult to explain the feelings you have when your horse

does master a new skill particularly if he had had a problem understanding your request. It's magic!

I am often asked 'what is voice training?' Well, over the years it does appear that the importance of the voice is being played down, you will even hear trainers say 'do not keep talking to your horse!' In fact voice training is the basis for this book. For us the voice is the main communication line to the horse. Horses have the most amazing memories so give them a chance to use them. Try thinking about the words that you use to your horse in a normal situation, are there many and do they mean anything to your horse?

We build up our vocabulary past the point of the everyday words and we do this for two reasons. Firstly because of the variety of work that we do with our horses such as displays, television and stage work when it is important for them to understand our verbal requests. Secondly, it works – we train all horses to the voice because it does help.

However, you will see that I have taken it even further with Jack who really is the most gifted horse and he is not yet finished. Even though at this point in his training I am very confident that I can work him anywhere, I was brought back down to earth at a lecture demonstration. For the first time I took one of the stallions along to show how we start Western. Jack opened up the demo doing his routine and although he was going very well I felt he wasn't quite with me, he appeared a little sluggish and his ears were behaving like antennae.

I pointed out to the audience that Jack was not yet finished in his training and if there was a problem I would show them how we would take remedial action, by taking him back a step. Well, what can I say but after I stripped all the tack off and sent him away he did three movements spot on, then came into halt. When I asked him to go 'back' he literally stood and looked at me with a very insolent look. The audience roared with laughter, I tried again and got the same response! It's very important to keep 'cool' and not to worry about the hundreds of people who are watching you and waiting to see how you cope with your horse refusing to do what he is asked. So I smiled and then set about showing them the correction, which was to bring in an assistant to help him to step backwards. I was perturbed though when he threw another no response at me when I asked him to pirouette. By this time everyone thought it was a great laugh.

Finally we got to the end of the programme and suddenly I heard the creator of our problems. My mother, who works with me at these demonstrations had already pointed out to the audience that if something is so out of character for a horse, such as we were seeing with Jack then it is really important to find the cause. Was he tired from the long journey, did he have a colic attack coming? At this point the stallion Illustre suddenly neighed very loudly. It would appear that because Illustre could not see the horses who had travelled up with him and then Jack had moved out of sight, he was sending out distress calls telling them to come back to him, just as he would do in the wild! So while Jack was with me physically, mentally he was back with the stallion. Nature was stronger than me at that point in time!

It does not matter how old your horse is, think of him as a blank book when starting any work if he has not done it before. The art of training is to produce your horse in a manner so that he loses none of his own natural spirit. You must present what you want him to learn clearly so

that he understands and basically you show him what to do. Your voice is your biggest asset. Teach him his words. If your horse is panicking you can calm him down, it can be used either in a tone that will praise him, get him moving forward or get his attention if he is not listening to you.

As I have said, all our horses are trained in this manner and that includes racehorses. We started our own horse Damarita in our normal way. When I took her to the racing yard as a three-year-old ready for work, I explained all the work we had done with her and they smiled at us, maybe thinking we were not for real when I said that when I talk to her she knows her words. Still the time spent on the preparation work paid off, she was happy to settle anywhere in the string and went into the starting stalls calmly and waited for the off. The trainer was very surprised at her whole attitude and said that if only more of the horses were sent in as well prepared as she was then the job would be so much easier. Mind you the jockey was even more surprised when I told him that when he was ready to go not to use the whip, but that he should kick her on and say 'faster Snowy'. He had to take the smile off his face. Unfortunately he left her too much to do, but he could not believe how she responded to his voice to finish a close third!

When training, the first thing you have to do is to teach your horse to learn. You must open the door to your horse's mind. The very first movement that your horse responds to, no matter how small, is a breakthrough to building up your own communication line. Give him plenty of praise. He is learning to learn and you are over the first hurdle. Carry on with the same approach for all the new movements you are showing him to do, treat all as if they are the first.

CAN MY HORSE OR PONY LEARN VOICE TRAINING AND LIBERTY WORK?

Realistically any horse or pony no matter what their size or age can learn this work. My international horse Salute learned the Spanish Walk at sixteen years of age! What needs to be remembered most importantly though is that horses, like humans, do not all learn at the same rate. In a group of children it is very rare that they will all progress at the same speed, some may shine in one direction others in a different one. Yet it is up to the teacher to keep a happy balance and the ones who are slower must not be made to feel that they are no good because they will then lose their confidence.

Often horses which learn quickly are what we would call 'sharp'. Take Jack who is by nature a laid-back relaxed type of horse but he is very intelligent. When he is fresh he starts offering you movements or giving something he thinks you want. Being overzealous can be a problem and when it comes to him doing the changes across the school he tries to get as close to you as possible! With this type of character you have to be very careful that they do not start anticipating the work, in other words starting the movement before you ask for it. If this happens, do not panic, simply make him wait for your verbal aid and be very positive and clear with the aids and with the position of your body and the whip. It is imperative that you do not let him set the agenda otherwise you will find that he will end up getting out of control, cutting corners and simply not listening to you. If necessary get an assistant to lead him or you can put a rider back on and this will make it easier for you to re-establish the ground rules.

Sometimes it is easier to work with a horse which is a bit quiet and slow. It might take

Our first New Sensations day and Tom Tom, Sam and Boysie are meeting their handlers for the first time. All ages and sizes (both equines and human) can learn this work.

longer for him to learn but do not get depressed, he will eventually get the idea of what you are asking him to do. It is important that you do not try to rush and hurry him because he will start to make mistakes and then he will lose his confidence. The good thing about this type of horse is that what he learns stays in his memory and he does not normally give you any cause for concern.

LESSON 1

THE EQUIPMENT AND HOW TO USE IT

THE TACK

Before the introduction of the bum bag I always kept the titbits in my pockets, much to the disgust of my mother when she used to do my washing! If I hadn't used all the goodies I often forgot to take them out – boiled carrots and stewed apple took on a whole new meaning.

When starting a young or fresh horse I think it is a good idea to wear a riding hat and I always wear gloves. For the horse you need a good lunge line which is not too light in the hand and is full length. Your horse can wear a snaffle bridle, it does not matter what type of bit you normally ride in, he needs to work either in a snaffle with a link underneath which clips to both sides of the bit thereby making it easy to change across, or a headcollar (with the lunge attached to the back ring) or a very well-fitting cavesson.

You can use any well-fitting saddle or a good roller and you will need side-reins. It is best if your horse wears either boots or bandages when learning as a precaution just in case he turns quickly and bangs himself.

HANDLING THE LUNGE WHIP

I always stress that before you start lungeing you should know how to handle a lunge whip. It is very important to be comfortable handling the lunge whip, making sure that you are happy with the weight in your hand and even more importantly that you can place the end of the lash where you need to. If necessary, practise throwing the lash so that you are able to place it anywhere.

Watch any expert working with a whip and one thinks that it is no problem. When I was a young whipper-snapper in the circus, the knife thrower made it look so easy cutting the pages of paper in half with his bull whip. I decided that my friend and I were going to learn the act, with me handling the whip. Luckily my friend insisted that I practised on my own before I did the paper trick with her holding it. What can I say? In an effort to get it to crack not only did I wrap the whip around me but I nearly took my ear off in the process! I gave that up as a bad job and have not lifted a bull whip since.

Cavesson

Headcollar

Snaffle and link

Nicola and I see who can touch the bag first! It was the best of three with the loser buying lunch! The aim is to do the same exercise with a tin can.

THE REASON FOR THE WHIP

The whip is your directive aid and you might need to just touch him on the shoulder to keep him out when he is learning as well as giving him the verbal aid or even touch him on the hock to encourage more activity. We train our horses to come to the whip and never be afraid of it. When we were doing an advertisement where the horse had to be loose in the field with no tack, he had to come when called and rear on his hind legs, the whip was important to him because it is his guider. When a horse is rearing he cannot see the person on the ground directing him. By holding the whip high in front of him he could see and follow it. He would only come down when the whip was dropped and he was given the verbal aid.

Sometimes people try to send their horse away with the end of the lunge line. This is not really the best thing to use for this type of work because the whip is an extension of your arm and as it is ridged it is much easier to handle and place the second you might feel that your horse needs directional assistance.

THE WORKING ROUND

As you can see from our photographs, we have a variety of arenas we use including the white plastic fencing-round which I also use at my demonstrations and which was made to my design. One of my first rounds was made of straw bales, two bales high covered in plastic so it was waterproof and the horses couldn't catch their feet in the string. It was secured around the outside with rope and stakes. You can really use anything as long as it is safe and secure, wooden pallets also appear to work, the height can be three feet (1m) and do make sure you can close your gateway off. The flooring you use should obviously be safe and non-slip and there are many products on the market. Sometimes good mediums can be found locally. The problem with just using a grass surface, is that it will not be a consistent footing throughout the seasons although we do practise on it at times. The diameter we work in is normally forty-two feet (13m) which I find to be a comfortable space.

The first time I worked Laddie off the lunge at a demo was rather embarrassing to say the least. At the time I did not have my own portable round so the people kindly put up a straw one for me. Being very confident as one must be at these dos, I let Laddie off the lunge explaining to the audience that this would show how much he was listening to me. With that he trotted off and went straight out over the bales, then he decided that he couldn't find his way back in when called until we made an opening for him! He went back on the lunge for the rest of the demo – obviously he was not quite ready to go free.

LESSON 2

GETTING READY FOR WORK

TACKING UP

It is possible that you have not lunged your horse before, so I will take it from the beginning. Tie your horse up while you are getting him ready. Put on the saddle or roller and attach the side-reins to the side, about midway or bottom-of-saddle-flap level, and fix the free ends so they do not hang down and bang your horse's legs. Talk to your horse when you are doing this, give his ears a rub and see if you can gauge how he is feeling. I will just take one step back here; if your horse has not yet been ridden and you are just starting him, then you do have some basic foundation points to cover. He needs to have been wearing a mouthing bit for a period of time and to be comfortable with it, he should be wearing a roller and breast plate day and night, until he is well accustomed to them, then add a rug when you are happy with everything. You can then replace the roller with a saddle for work.

Even though I have suggested that it is best to tie up your horse when getting ready and leave him tied up to wait for you, with young horses who are being mouthed and backed I do leave them loose in their stable after they have been tacked up with a breast plate and saddle. They have some treats in the manger to give them something else to think about. I find this all helps to put them at ease with moving around with the tack on. I always remove the reins and stirrups so they cannot get caught up; someone told me once that their horse managed to get his hoof trapped in the stirrup and was in quite a state when they found him.

Put on the boots or bandages (you should already have checked his legs over when you cleaned him off) and finally put on whatever headgear he is wearing and make sure it fits correctly. If it is a bridle take off the reins unless you are using a rider to assist in which case place the reins over the neck then twist them underneath the throat and thread the throat lash through to secure them. Your horse is now ready and waiting to be brought out to work. Lead him out with the lunge but do not attach the side reins to the bit whilst your horse is in the stable, for safety reasons wait until you are in your working area. Either carry the whip out with you or put it out in the working area beforehand. Depending on the time of year remember to put on the fly repellent.

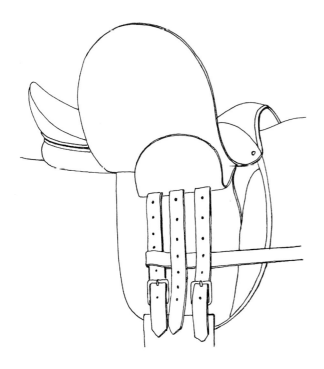

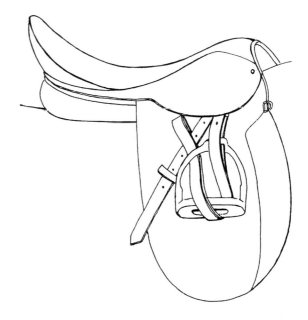

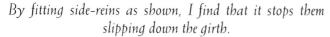

By fitting side-reins as shown, I find that it stops them slipping down the girth.

If you are leaving the stirrups on secure them as shown.

LEADING YOUR HORSE OUT

When walking your horse out make sure that he is up beside you and not walking too close – you should be no further back than his shoulder. He should not be allowed to get into the position where he is walking along behind you because it is not a safe practice. Do not let him pull you along, if he does, just give a positive feel down the lunge and say his name then 'steady'. The minute he responds ease the pressure and give him praise. It is not good for any horse to get into the habit of rushing out or back to the stable. I practise asking him to stand quietly and wait then walk

on, beware though of holding any words written as gospel, this is where you must use your own initiative. If the weather is cold and my horse very much up on his toes going out, I would not want to set up a possible problem by saying 'right lad, stand still'. However when he is going to the field for a loose run no matter what the weather, he is not allowed just to go free once inside. I always turn him around. I give him something non-choking to eat and keep talking to him while I slide the lunge off. I tell him 'no wait' followed when ready by 'all right away'. Then he goes. But I would practise halting on the way back from the field.

When letting him loose in the field, don't make the mistake that I made once only. I was in a hurry and rushing, so as I let the horse go I turned my back on him. Fortunately for me the next thing I felt rushing past my ears was only the wind, as one hoof literally went each side of my head. To say I was shaken was an understatement.

THE WORKING AREA

It is not conducive to good training in the beginning to have a lot of distractions around, if your horse is not already used to them. It is possible they may distract him and cause him to lose concentration. It is your job to make sure you give your horse the best chance to work with you.

We have plastic bags hanging around our pen, our horses go in the pen for a roll or leg stretch, even if it is windy. They are well used to the bags billowing and blowing around and they know they will not eat them! I often place things in the pen with a horse when he is just in there for a play, such as a sheet of plastic on the ground with some horse nuts on it.

ENTERING THE WORKING AREA

If you are using a pole as your gate make sure that you have it moved out of the way when leading your horse in, replacing it once inside. He needs to learn that he never crosses over the pole when it forms part of the boundary even if it is on the floor.

Walk your horse into the centre of your work place, do not forget to use your voice and tell him to stand. The choice is yours as to what words you use but it is very important that you always use the same words. He should not fidget or turn around; if he does just quietly insist both verbally and with a feel on the lunge so he realises that he needs to listen to you and wait for the next request. Give praise when you get a response, do not forget that it is not a good idea to keep giving titbits or you can get into the situation where he keeps looking for food all the time. A rub on his face or a pat on the neck is fine with a 'good boy'. If for any reason you are having a problem getting your horse to stand still, practise doing it by something solid or on the outside track as this way he has less escape routes. Beware of pulling your horse in a circle around you, this becomes a bad habit very quickly. Use the right hand to keep his head and neck straight with the lunge. Lift your left hand up and forward at the same time saying 'no, stand'. Slowly increase the time you ask him to wait.

THE REASON FOR AND CORRECT POSITION OF SIDE-REINS

The side-reins are to help your horse to concentrate on you, which in turn gives you more control. They stop the horse from turning his head to look at something that might have caught his eye and also help him to balance because of the way he will carry himself. Where you place the side-reins will depend on your horse's head and neck carriage. As a guide, do not go any lower than the bottom of the saddle flap but try the area in between to find the most comfortable position for your horse. Do not put

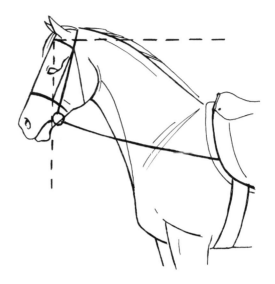

a) too tight

b) too loose

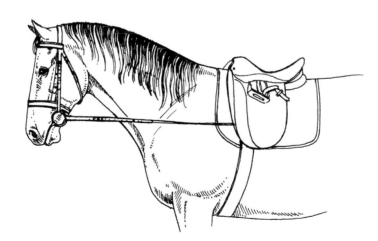

c) correct

The three actions of the side-reins

them down any lower on the saddle or the roller as this will only encourage him to go onto the forehand, possibly making him drop his head and neck too low. This is incorrect and can become a bad habit.

There are two schools of thought regarding the fitting of the side-reins – whether to have them equal or shorter on the inside. To be honest I work both ways depending on the horse and what I am wanting to achieve with him. In this type of work it is best to keep them level because you do not want to keep stopping your horse whilst you are altering the reins.

FITTING THE SIDE-REINS

Make sure that the side-reins are not put on too tightly. The guide is that the horse's nose should be either just on or in front of the vertical. If your horse has never worn side-reins before, you may need to have them a little looser than normal in the beginning as there is the risk of his panicking and running backwards. When your horse accepts them, take them up a little if he has not really worked in the correct manner, in other words accepting the bit and carrying himself in a balanced way. Be very careful that you do not work him for too long, otherwise he will get sore and stiff. You will need to build up your working time as he develops his muscles.

LOOSENING UP YOUR HORSE

It is important to remember that even though you are not riding your horse he should still work correctly, so if your horse is stiff it would

be in his best interest to do some loosening and stretching exercises in the stable everyday. To encourage him to loosen and stretch his neck place him by the wall so that his quarters cannot move. Then tempt him with a carrot so that he brings his neck round to you. Start within his reach then move the carrot back so that he stretches his neck and relating muscles. To flex his joints lift up each of the front legs and stretch slowly forward. In this way your horse is having his muscles loosened. Also lift his hind legs up and stretch them slowly forwards. Remember the voice through all this.

Work him on the lunge with lots of transitions to loosen him up before you move on to the basic exercise work. I would then use the side-reins shorter on the inside and alter them when changing the rein. When you have progressed to working with two reins you can also use this as a way of loosening up a stiff horse before putting him on the lunge. By feeling on the inside rein you are asking him to bend in and he stretches the outside muscles. Do remember to do this on both reins but be careful to watch that he does not just follow his nose and come in off the circle. You need to develop a good outside hand that allows him to bend but does not give away all the contact and you can ask him for a half halt so that he gets a clear directional aid. Do not forget the verbal aids. When you are happy with his way of going then progress to the next step working in the round and extending your horse's word index and movements.

Whilst I have said that one should not work with side-reins low, I must point out that professional trainers do sometimes use side-reins lower but it should not be in order to force the horse into a position. They are used to encourage the horse to use himself better and take an equal contact through to the bit. I have a

The rider must be inactive when on their horse, only assisting when asked. I often have the reins knotted so that the rider is not tempted to keep using the reins. It can get rather exciting as they fight their natural instinct to hold the reins!

roller which has rings in many working positions going from the top, which I use when I am wanting to work my horse up and more into self-carriage to lower ones which I find beneficial in the re-schooling of horses. Because the rings are lower it gives a different feel to the mouth and encourages the horse to drop his head and neck, which in turn helps to develop the muscles over his quarters, back and neck. This shows the horse how you want him to stretch and, as with everything you do, it will only help if used properly and it is only with time, patience and practice that you can learn how to do all that you are reading about.

THE RIDER OR LEADING ASSISTANT

If you have a rider assisting you, they must sit quietly on your horse holding the reins and only directing the horse with the minimum of aids. The same goes if you have an assistant leading your horse, they are only to help where needed. Obviously it will be more in the beginning but as time goes on your horse must be allowed to take the initiative when he offers. On no account must anyone else speak to your horse during the training sessions except you, he must be focused on you and waiting for your next direction.

A problem that I have occasionally encountered when using a rider is that they find it difficult sometimes to just sit on the horse and follow him as he starts to take the initiative when he begins to understand what is being asked. Another problem that arises is one that I have as well, which is that I mix up my right and left, this really shows when lifting the legs or doing turns.

Do not worry if you do not have help, it is not impossible to do this work on your own – it might just take a little longer. All that I am writing is relevant by whichever method you decide to use with your horse.

LESSON 3

BASIC EXERCISES EXPLAINED

Before you try any of the advanced work with your horse, both of you have to master the basics which are quite simply the foundation to this work. One of the first things you must be able to do is that when you call your horse's name, followed with 'come here' or 'halt', he will respond from wherever he is. You will then start to build up the vocabulary between you and your horse.

THE VOICE

As I have said, your voice is everything in this work, with all the verbal directions be aware of how you are talking to your horse. The aids must be soft and drawn out, not sharp and abrupt. As your horse is learning this work he may not understand, he may not respond or will do the wrong thing. Simply repeat the request again. You may need to move closer to him to help him do what you are asking. When the horse knows the work use the stronger tone (do not shout) as a correction only if you do not get a response from your first request.

The voice really does work with all animals. Many years ago the elephants with whom my father had worked and knew well were sent to the continent to take part in the film *Cleopatra*. We had left the circus at this point and received an urgent phone call for Dad to go to the elephants which were running riot and not listening to their handler. It had got to the point where the handmaidens who the elephants were supposed to be carrying with their trunks were being dropped everywhere, and the hand-maidens had decided to go on strike! Anyway Dad arrived and Mary the matriarch elephant (the boss) heard Dad before she saw him but she recognised his voice – it was one she knew and respected. After that things went swimmingly.

LUNGE AND WHIP CONTROL

Make sure that the lunge is looped correctly when being held. I tend to keep the lunge in the same hand when working on either rein. It is up to you to do whichever you find easier, you may prefer to keep changing the lunge rein and whip

over when you change the direction. Never put your hand through the loop or wrap the lunge around your hand and wrist, this is asking for trouble.

Before we actually start, just a word about whip positions and lunge handling which you need to remember otherwise it can be confusing for your horse and yourself. When working, try to think of your position as forming a triangle from your horse's nose back to you and to his quarters. The four main positions are: (1) pointing the whip to your horse's rear end to move your horse forward giving the aid 'forwards' at the same time; (2) whip to the shoulder to keep your horse out, with the aid 'out' at the same time; (3) to slow down or steady up raise the whip in front of your horse's head saying to him 'steady' or 'whoa'; and (4) to halt, as well as bringing the whip to the front, step sideways so both the whip and you are in front of the horse's eye, giving the aid 'halt' at the same time. Before each verbal aid I will say his name or 'listen' as this gets his attention and he knows that something is about to happen, in other words a verbal half halt.

You need to keep the lunge line well off the floor and when your horse is going around you check how you are feeling in your body. What I mean by that statement is, check that your arms and shoulders are not tight or stiff, otherwise your horse might start pulling against you if he feels that you are 'dead' on the end of the lunge.

It is worth taking the time to practise with the lunge before you have a horse on the end of it – it is easy to get in a muddle when the horse is coming into you and you cannot get the lunge out of the way quickly enough. Keep the whip hand still and only move the other one.

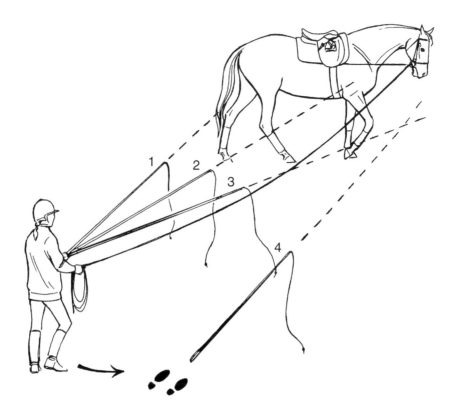

Whip positions   1 forward   2 out   3 steady   4 halt

When you are taking up the slack from the lunge you need to do it in either of the following ways. When bringing the horse to you, or you are approaching him, take the whip to the front underneath the lunge, lift your thumb and catch the lunge between it and the whip. To take up the slack, raise the thumb, draw the lunge arm back and when enough lunge is through to make a loop, close your thumb, bring the lunge arm forward to the whip hand and take up the loop. Simply repeat the process if needed. All the time move only your lunge arm and keep the whip hand still otherwise you will be giving the horse many conflicting directions!

THE FIRST MOVEMENT

The first movement your horse will learn is to move away from you and go off anti-clockwise on the left rein. Using my horse's name to get his attention, I then follow up with the verbal aid 'walk on, out'. Though you should stand in the middle of the circle and turn in a small space, if you are doing this on your own you might find that in the beginning you will need to walk out towards your horse as you are sending him away. At the same time feed out the lunge so that you allow him to go in the direction you are asking for; make sure that you do not get in front of his

eye line or he might stop. With the whip in your right hand keep it pointed to his shoulder, then move it to the driving position and say 'walk on out' and praise him until he is out on the edge of the round. Whatever work you do in the round always keep your eyes on your horse's quarters. Do not make the mistake of taking him for granted even if he is dead quiet! Repeat your verbal aid and praise him when he gets to the desired point, make sure that he keeps up a positive walk. Watch him throughout the movement and be ready just in case he tries to turn back to you, if he does, just a short flick either towards or on the shoulder with the words 'no, out' should be enough to deter him. Praise him when he responds to your directive.

If I have a student who thinks they know it all, I will put them in the pen to lunge Jack. He is brilliant at putting them in their place. Sometimes horses become automated and drilled when they are lunged a lot, they do what is asked even if it is incorrect. However, Jack will assess them as they try to move him out. For instance, unless they stand behind his eye line and by his shoulder he will not move out, instead he will keep turning in on them and refusing to move out!

HALTING WHEN ASKED

Let him walk around for a few times so that he is balanced and listening, then you are going to prepare him to halt. Every time you are going to ask your horse to do a movement remember to warn him with his name or the aid 'listen'. Once he understands this then his response will become quicker – it is the equivalent to the ridden half halt. So call his name to prepare him, and follow

this with your verbal aid of 'halt'. At the same time give a feel down the lunge, moving the whip and your body in a definite movement to the front of him, so you are in front of his eye line. If he does not respond, just repeat the whole process. If you are on your own and find that he just does not understand what you are asking, then simply shorten up the lunge and walk towards him whilst he is still circling. Bring the whip to the front again, feel on the lunge, repeat his name then say 'halt'; it does not matter if you get quite close to him. Do this a few times then leave it. Gradually build up the distance between you when you give the aid. Sometimes it does take a little while to be able to coordinate it all together but practice makes perfect.

It is important that your horse learns to halt on the outside track and is not allowed to turn in. Your helper can give him a pat on the neck while you give verbal praise, during this time your whip and you must stay in the halt position. Only when you are ready to walk on do you step back to the working position in the centre, giving the aid 'walk on' whilst moving the whip to the rear position. Again, give praise when he responds. Practise this exercise a few times. On your last halt walk up to your horse, stay in front of his eye and keep repeating the verbal aid 'halt – good boy', when you reach him make a big fuss of him. I would also give him a treat.

Now you need to repeat this lesson on the other rein, and as he has not yet learnt to change the rein you should lead him into the middle from the track. At this point do not ask him to 'come here' because he needs to master the halt on the track first. Give him the warning then ask him to 'halt' while you get organised to move him off from the new direction. Some horses find it difficult to master movements on a different rein but, as with all lessons, quietly

For the halt I always bring the whip to the front and make a very clear step forward in front of the horse's eye line, at the same time giving the verbal aid. He is just coming into the halt here. Ideally his head and neck could have been a little lower.

insist. Make sure your verbal aid, the whip and body movements are making the request very clear.

You do not have to change the lunge rein from one hand to the other when your horse moves off in the new direction. He is now going off clockwise on the right rein and you keep the lunge in the left hand and whip in the right. When using the whip for an aid just move it under the lunge; again, practice does help.

Once you can do the above exercises well in walk and your horse is listening to you, then you can practise the transitions walk, trot, walk and halt.

IMPORTANT WORDS

Three of the most important phrases your horse will learn are firstly his name then the words 'come here' and 'halt' or 'stand'. Every time we speak to him in the stable, or anywhere, use his name, more often than not people will add 'good boy'.

It is very important that you pass on the words that you use to whoever is working with the horse or any animal for that matter. Dad used to take the racing camels around the country but before they hit the big time, the girls and I had to go down to Longleat Lion Reserve with Dad to start them off. Even though they were domestic and did rides they had to learn to race when asked. There were plenty of helpers shouting and making noises behind and with us encouraging our mounts to go on the words 'allez, allez', it was a pretty exciting sight to see us all galloping down the long verge. The only problem was that I forgot to tell one of the girls that to stop our mounts all we had to say was 'whoa'. We stopped on command but she kept going. All I heard was 'stop, stop'. I will not repeat her words to me when she finally returned. The most printable ones were 'never again Larrigan'.

BRINGING HIM TO YOU

When you have halted your horse on the outside track walk to within six feet (two metres) of him, take up the slack in your lunge and re-loop as you go. While you are approaching him praise him and repeat the verbal aid 'halt'. To bring him to you, bring the whip across your body and, at the same time, say his name followed by 'come

here'. Giving a feel down the lunge will encourage him to you. Keep facing him and when he comes to you make much of him with a lot of verbal praise and patting, now keep taking steps backwards and keep asking him to come to you. Halt him a few times while you are still facing him. Say his name, then give the verbal aid 'halt'. I tend to lift my hand up in front as well. Make much of him every time he responds to you, give him a reward sometimes. You are teaching him to follow you anywhere in different directions, while you are walking backwards and asking him to come to you.

This is a movement that many horses start to anticipate so beware, do not always call him in from the halt on the track.

One day I was doing a photographic session with Jack in the field, and I asked the photographer to stand behind me so he could get the shots of Jack galloping to me when I called and clapped my hands. I called Jack and he came at full speed towards me and went straight past stopping dead in front of the petrified photographer. We have a great shot of me with my arms open and Jack flying past. Not quite what we were after – but that's life!

THE MOVE OFF

After calling him into you, you must send him away in the new direction (the right rein). From facing your horse in the front position step back to his offside shoulder and face the shoulder, with the whip in your right hand point it to the shoulder and ask him to walk on. Walk a few steps with him if needed, move the whip to the driving position at the rear and then turn to the

right making sure you are feeding out the lunge to allow him to go.

When you find that he is responding well, start to increase the distance from where you call him to you. Eventually you should stand still in the middle of the round and your aids will be to say his name then swing the whip across your front and call him to you. Initially keep the whip horizontal but as he progresses in training let the end down to the ground. Still practise walking backwards and bringing him with you.

DIRECTION CHANGE

At this point you and your horse have nearly mastered the basics and he should know his name, the commands 'halt', 'walk on' and 'come here'. You will now work on the change and for this your horse will come across in front of you and change direction to the other rein.

This can get a bit exciting when your horse is learning the movement and you have to be quite quick at taking up the slack in the lunge during the change and then allowing your horse to go the other way! At the same time do not forget to watch those hindquarters.

We will start on the left rein and the verbal aid you will give your horse is 'change'. Your movements are as follows: keep the horse walking, call his name to prepare him followed by the words 'come here' and 'change'. Take the whip across your body but wider than if you wanted him to halt, draw him to you and take up the lunge as he approaches you. You do not want him to misunderstand the next part of the movement so it must be very clear that he should cross in front of you to change the direction. Just

The change of rein right to left. (Top left) I call his name, say 'change' and take up the lunge. (Top right) As he comes in, the whip is to my right. (Bottom left) I step to my right and bring the whip towards his shoulder and say 'out'. (Bottom right) I repeat 'change' and allow him to go in the new direction (in this instance he has cut in, I repeated 'out' and pointed the whip to the shoulder).

before he reaches you walk quietly towards his offside, the whip still across your front and gently touch him on the off shoulder. By doing this and repeating the 'change' aid and 'walk on, out' you will encourage him to move forward and past you thereby changing direction. Be quick to allow the lunge out so that you do not catch him in the mouth.

Repeat this movement a few times on each rein. Be careful not to always do this movement in the same spot, it is important that he is listening to you and not just doing it through association with the place. With all the movements that your horse is learning do not progress from one to the next until he is listening and is confidently doing what is asked.

WHIP TRAINING

I cannot stress enough that it is of the utmost importance that your horse is never punished with the whip, nor should he be worried or frightened when the whip is around him. You must take into account your horse's temperament and what had been done to him before he came to you. For instance, if he had been abused or if he is a nervous type, you must make allowances for him. Do not rush him with the whip work but gradually build up his confidence and trust. Take your time to stroke and touch him all over with it, gently throwing it over, under and around his body. When you want to start to crack it hold it away from your horse and just make a soft sound first. If all is going well then you can make stronger noises with it. You need to treat everything you do calmly and quietly and slowly build up the foundations; if at any time your horse is worried simply retrace your steps. All the time use your voice to praise him, pat him and it would not hurt to give him some goodies – you want him to associate the whip and the noises with treats.

I had a phone call following a lecture demonstration at a local riding school. The owner said she was very pleased to hear all the children talking to the ponies but was rather concerned when she went into the indoor school to find one of the children being towed around by a pony on the lunge and another saying 'no make him stand while I crack the whip, where are the carrots?'

While working them, remember that our horses are our friends and it is cooperation not domination that will get the response back from them.

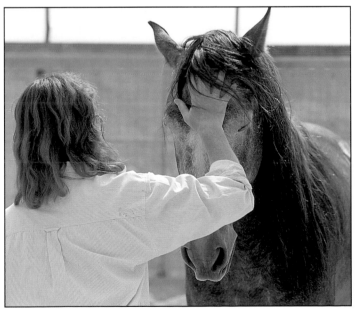

This is what your end result should be, no fear (top) and giving a reward (bottom).

LESSON 4

PROGRESSING WITH YOUR VOICE AND LUNGE WORK

Before you progress onto this work, you and your horse must be happy and able to go through the basics without any problems.

Your basic work should be done on both reins and when showing my horses new movements I will start them on different reins because this way they can learn two simultaneously.

THE PIROUETTE

We will start with the pirouette on the left rein and the movement is as follows. Following your directions the horse will do a 360 degree turn preferably spinning on his hocks or what I call 'a turn on the belly', in other words imagine yourself sitting on him and remaining still while his quarters and his shoulders move around in the same direction but you will stay in the same place. When he has finished you will be facing the same direction in which you started: this is the essence of the pirouette.

The easiest way to teach this movement is to have an assistant riding your horse. To prepare your horse to start this movement, stand him on the outside track with the rider up in order to assist you if needed. The rider should be holding the reins in both hands. All they need do is feel on the inside rein when you ask him to come round with your aid. As the horse starts to understand what is being asked, the rider does less and lets him do it on his own. Have the side-reins on and clip the lunge rein to the bit on the near side. Loop the lunge from the inside to the outside over the neck so that it comes back under the lower jaw to your hand. Ask the horse to 'halt' while you step back towards the centre.

The verbal aids I give are: his name, 'steady', and 'pirouette'. The body moves are as follows: take your whip across your front throwing the lash out as far as possible to the left. At the same time step to your left – as the rider is showing the horse the way around – and at the moment the horse is a facing you bring the whip across your front and step two steps to the right, now you need him to finish the turn so you bring the whip to the right and then just throw the end towards him. During the whole turn the rider just uses the inside rein to bring him round in as tight a turn as possible. Your rider will have to be

very quick to lift the lunge from behind them and, as you can see, coordination features for all concerned. When he has completed the turn ask him to halt and make much of him.

If you have assistance on the ground, the assistant needs to have a short lunge on the nearside bit ring and should stand back facing the horse's hip, so they can watch his quarters. You have your lunge on as before and give the same aids. Your assistant will bring the horse around and at the same time keep their lunge taut and consequently the horse will follow the assistant around. Ask the horse to halt and make much of him.

Finally to do this movement on your own, make the outside side-rein longer so that when your horse is brought around, the outside rein will not give him a conflicting message. Put the lunge on in the manner already explained. Because of his positioning of his neck you will not be able to walk many straight strides before commencing the pirouette. Ask him to walk on, use all the required aids and feel on the lunge, as he is already bent he will just follow the indication on the bit. When he has completed the movement halt him and make much. After he is doing the movement when asked, make sure the side-reins are even.

With any of the above methods only practise twice on each rein. Your horse must first master this movement at the walk and, when fully happy and 'safe' in it, then progress to the trot.

Louise is bringing Jack around (top) then lifts the lunge well clear (middle) but (bottom) got a bit carried away and pulled it clean out of my hand. Things do not always go right, however it didn't bother Jack!

THE VOLTE

The volte is where you walk towards your horse and he performs a small circle around you, as he completes the volte you step back to the centre and he carries on. This is a very easy movement to start, with or without help. So that my horses do not confuse this with the pirouette I tend to work off the right rein. The verbal aids are 'steady, here, volte'. As I say 'steady' I move the whip across my front, walk towards my horse's quarters and take up the lunge slack, which in turn brings the horse around me and at which point I turn on the spot to follow him round. On completion of the volte I move the whip forward and say 'good boy, out'. Then I step back towards the centre, at the same time feeding the lunge out so he stays on the track. Ask him to halt and make much of him.

I do, however, sometimes cheat with this exercise. While I am asking my horse to volte and if he looks as if he is not too sure I pull out a carrot and wave it under his nose while I keep turning, repeating the words 'volte, here'. It never fails with Jack.

REIN BACK

One movement in particular that I find the horses sometimes anticipate when starting to learn it is the rein back. When they are asked to halt they start to move back straight away and it is very important to say 'no, wait, stand'. When he is settled, ask again and aim for it to be a controlled stepping back. If you have a horse that goes backwards when you do not want him to, he is learning an evasion, this is called napping.

One horse that was sent to me for retraining had this problem. He did not have any physical reasons as to why he went backwards when his owner asked him to leave other horses. I decided to try the natural method, so I set up the situation in which I knew the problem would occur. I had deliberately planned it not far away from a nice large holly bush! The remedy worked because this horse had only started to test his rider with this evasion so it was not ingrained and he had given himself a prickly fright.

Your horse should have learnt to go back on request in the stable. When working in the round I ask them to go back by my staying in the centre but facing the same direction as my horse, I then tell him 'back'. At the same time I step back. To start this movement ask your horse to halt on the outside track, praise him and walk up to him; facing the same direction as him, place your nearest hand on his chest whilst giving a gentle push with your hand or thumb, telling him 'back'. If you do not get a response with that, then place your left hand on the headcollar, the right hand can hold the whip in front of his chest and just taps him, while you repeat the verbal aid. The moment your horse responds praise him, then repeat.

PUSHING

Now you will see how I go about training my horses to do a 'trick'. However, even though Jack has learnt to push me with his head, it is worth remembering that police horses are trained to push people with their bodies when used for crowd control work and it can be useful for gate work, as you will see in the Western section.

This is very easy to do even without an assistant. Stand on the track with your horse directly behind you. I put on side-reins to help direct him and he cannot turn his head away. Either split the reins or use a rope on each side of the bit and hold one in each hand. Stand about one foot (30cm) in front of him facing the way you are going to be pushed. When you are ready tell him to 'push', at the same time bring him forward to your lower back. As his nose makes contact with you move forward and give plenty of praise. Once he has learnt the word then I should be able to apply it to anything, a door, a gate or even knocking me over!

Whenever you are teaching your horse something new, always keep your eyes in the back of your head particularly with this trick. When finishing a demo with Jack I asked him to stand and wait in the middle of the round while I went to pick up something off the floor and with that I bent down. The next thing I knew I was flat on my back on the floor and he was standing over me waiting for his mint. I learnt my lesson very quickly. I always keep one eye on him now and turn my back very carefully.

THE SPANISH WALK

The Spanish Walk or March is a movement which is not normally used when working a horse at liberty but I do use it so I felt you should know how to train it correctly. It is a very good exercise for horses which are tight in the shoulders, which in turn can affect the paces. Also I have noticed that more people are bringing in Iberian horses who are either doing or learning this work but unfortunately it is not always being ridden properly. As with any work,

when done badly it can actually damage the horse. Equally, it is not a good idea to train your horse certain things if he is going to be sold because new riders can give conflicting aids and upset the horse.

Whilst learning this work it is important that the horse works correctly and for the finished picture of the Spanish Walk the horse should be accepting the bit and moving forward with his hind legs. It is totally incorrect for the horse to be above the bit and consequently hollowing his back and not allowing his hind legs to come through.

To prepare for this work I use a roller and side-reins and to this I have a lunge to the bit and I use a short whip. Standing my horse up against the fence on the left rein I tap the foreleg as high as possible, rather like an irritating fly. Find the most sensitive place for a reaction from the forearm up to the point of shoulder. The idea is to get your horse to lift when he feels the whip touch him. I also say 'left lift' and he must be praised for any response and walked on. I find that they start to paw the ground as soon as they are touched so it is very important that they walk on when asked, sometimes I will just touch them on the girth area as I ask them to walk on. To work on the other leg I change the rein and this helps to avoid confusion which can be caused by putting the whip across the horse's chest. Once the legs are raised on request on both reins in a good forward-going manner I then ask for the leg to be lifted every other stride. So it is left, left, or right, right. When this is established, staying on one rein I go for left, right, left. I then simply build up the strides. To ride this I give diagonal aids, for the left leg I feel down the left rein, apply pressure with the right leg and initially say 'left'. Be very aware of doing strange movements with the hands and legs. The

rider should always be quiet and still in the saddle. This work can also be done on the long reins.

This takes me back many years when I first started competing in dressage with Rainbeau, my mother's high school horse. I qualified for the ride-off in the Derby class and the four finalists had to ride each other's horses. I had a great time but one rider in particular threw the reins at me after her ride on Beau and made it clear she thought our training left something to be desired. Why? Very simply, instead of being

THE STRETCH

The stretch is another very good exercise for the shoulders and the back and I have already explained how you get your horse onto word commands if he is offering you something which you feel is beneficial to him. I have seen children who have taught their ponies to do this with food, granted it was not the perfect stretch but with a little knowledge things could be improved. Some horses just love doing some things though. Salute learnt this exercise in days and he became quite a show-off with it. In a prize-giving at an international competition when the Duchess of Richmond was presenting us with our rosette, he kept on stretching! He wouldn't listen to me – he was enjoying the applause so much. As with anything your horse is trained to do there are some very important guidelines to remember. Do not train your horse in his stable, with the exception of the words I have already mentioned. These are part of his stable management training. The stable is his own personal space where he can relax. Once your horse has learnt something do not be tempted to keep showing it off to everyone who comes to see him, that is very unfair on him.

If your horse becomes upset or agitated during this exercise it is possible that he is hurting, even though when you see him moving nothing looks wrong with his way of going. He might have a restriction somewhere that is causing him pain, if you have any doubts do not ask him to do this exercise.

Think of it in this manner. You felt all right before you started doing certain exercises, then you were made to do something that you found difficult. In doing so you 'tweaked' or agitated an old injury. Our horses cannot tell us 'ouch, watch out', we have to read their thoughts and be aware

This is how little response to expect when starting. Without the correct tack, Jack (above) is also putting his head too low which could become a habit and create a problem. I was trying this out but we are looking for a finished movement such as Idolo's (left), however all the credit goes to his owner for training him so well and his own talent for doing it.

subtle and asking Beau softly her aids were hard and demanding which he did not like or understand. Instead of trot he stayed in passage and the more she asked him to go forward the higher his passage became. In the walk her hands were too heavy on the reins and Beau did not like it and so he insisted on doing the Spanish Walk as his evasion. The rider was getting redder and redder in the face. The lesson from this is that it is not easy to ride trained horses, remember to ask not demand.

Here you can see that Jack is standing over a lot of ground and is just starting to stretch down towards my hand, at the same time I am giving him the voice aid 'stretch'.

of what is happening. This is the only problem with books, we can only describe what to look for. It could even be your horse just saying 'no'. I can't tell you which is which without seeing what is happening and this is something only experience can help you with but you must learn to interpret what your horse is telling you and what you are seeing. It is far better on these occasions to be considered 'easy' on your horse than the other way. You should never have to have a battle with any horse in order to get him to do what you are asking.

To start the stretch the natural way, the horse needs to wear his working tack with loose side-reins which help to keep him straight. I make sure that my horse will stand still when asked. I walk around him and run my hands down his legs, I do not want him to pick them up just because I touch them and if he does I simply say 'no, stand up' praising him when he does, this is important as later on you will have to pick up his leg and place it in a different position. Before you can show him the stretch he needs to learn to stand rather like a rocking horse, this will enable him to bring his head down through his knees. Touch behind the elbow, at the same time saying 'stretch', and move the front legs forward. You can either lift and then place his feet in the position you want or touch behind the fetlock with the end of the stick, or your foot, and he will move the leg forward away from it. Whichever method is used be quick and tell him to 'stand', and be very quick with your praise. When he settles ask him again to 'stretch'. It is quite possible that he will only manage a few inches at a time without fidgeting – it does not matter, let him settle and give him plenty of praise. As he gets confident with what you are asking and as his body lets the muscles go he will manage more. Once he is standing over a fair

amount of ground in a calm and static way then he is ready to proceed with the next part of the training.

Start with him standing square but have the lunge line loosely between his front legs with some food ready and accessible, then ask him to 'stretch down' touching him behind the elbow. When he has covered the ground repeat the verbal aid and direct his nose towards the food which you are holding behind his front legs. Remember only ask for a little stretch at a time whilst he is down, praise him and talk to him in a soothing voice, if there is anyone around you they must keep quiet. You must say 'all right, up' to signal the end of the exercise. It is important that you watch your horse and tell him before he starts to lift up, otherwise you will find that he will come up when he wants to.

PICK UP

This trick is a fun one but I do actually use it in everyday life with Jack who has great fun with his rubber feed bowl and it normally ends up at the back of his stable. So while I lean on his door I point to the bowl and say 'pick up Jack, here'. If it is upside down he takes a little while to right it, then he brings it to me. He loves praise but food is even better! I have to be careful that he does not drop the bowl in his effort to get to the mints!

In the same way that not every dog is cut out to be a police dog, do not take it personally if your horse looks at you with his mouth staying firmly shut if you offer him something to hold. I know I said earlier that we show our horses what to do but please do not take that literally in this case. Your friends might wonder what book you

Pick up

have been reading if they see you wandering around pointing to the bucket that you are carrying firmly by your teeth and showing to your horse! On the other hand I do know of one person who just might do that in desperation – no not me.

When I started this with Jack he got the hang of it very quickly – he is a very intelligent horse and he is by nature a 'mouthy' horse, always trying to nibble your jacket or devour your hand instead of the carrot! Anyone would think he was starving by his manner but certainly not by his appearance. In the end I decided to educate his mouth, so when I said 'stop' he would. However, nothing is allowed to be against his stable door because he takes it off and throws it down the yard.

HOW TO START HOLDING

Find a substance that your horse likes, rubber bowls appear interesting, a lightweight whip

even a jumper. It shouldn't be too thick. I put a headcollar on my horse and with one hand holding him steady I then offer him something to hold. Put it near his lips and tease him with it at the same time give the verbal aid 'hold' and as he takes it touch him under the chin with your fingers so he lifts his head up. Give him lots of praise then say 'all right, let go'. If he is not interested you could try putting something he likes around whatever you are trying to get him to hold, like a minty flavour.

DEVELOPING PICK UP

Once he is holding for you, then move on to picking up. Attach a rope to his headcollar, place whatever it is that you want him to pick up in an accessible position. Point to the object and direct his nose to it, saying 'pick up, here'. Follow up with 'hold' if you think he is going to let go, meanwhile bring him towards you with the rope. As with anything that your horse is

learning, do not expect him to hold the object for a long time, do not be greedy! It takes time and do not forget that you are now seriously expanding your Voice Training work. How many people can ask their horse to pick up and bring an object to them?

YOU THROW, HE CATCHES

Again this is you stretching your range of communication with your horse. I have a friend who is quite amazing with her horses. She has an act that has been passed down through the generations of her family. Would you believe she can throw a sugar cube from anywhere with her back to her horse and he will still catch it! That is a goal that I have for Jack and me. Mind you we cannot even do it with a carrot yet, so I am not sure how long it will take us to master that one!

I have two methods of teaching this. Don't laugh, but with one I tie a good sized carrot to a stick, then swing it to Jack. I think it goes at a speed that he can focus on and it appears to be working. Also I use a tea towel with mints tied into the corner but you can use whatever taste or smell appeals to your horse. You need to stand to the side of your horse's head and if necessary stand on a box otherwise you might get arm ache and find it difficult to do the next piece. You are aiming to get your horse to turn his head sideways. To do this hold the towel close to your horse's mouth on the near side. He should turn his head in order to reach the towel, if not then take hold of the headcollar and show him the towel. Give him a verbal aid while he is trying to get hold of the towel, play

with him so he cannot get his teeth into it straightway. Once he gets the taste into his mouth it makes life easier. It is a case of practice makes perfect – having time to work with your horse really does make all the difference. From there, move away a little and keeping hold of one end throw the tasty end towards him, giving the verbal aid 'catch' and when he tries to get it make a big fuss. So far Jack can catch the towel and he will wave with it.

PULLING AND RESISTING YOU

The reason I am telling you about these very different types of programme that you can do, is because I feel it is stretching you both mentally and in your word-association training. Also it might come in useful sometime when you least expect it, possibly out hacking.

After your horse is holding an object for as long as you ask him to then you can progress to teaching him word association for resisting and finally pulling you. Jack will hold the end of a rope while I hang on to my end, then we pull against each other so we are developing a tug of war type of game. Once your horse is holding when asked, simply keep a strong feel on what he is holding. You can then try and pull him towards you. Give plenty of praise however little the response. You need to build this up into a game and as he understands what you are showing him you can develop it. Allow him some slack, see if he will take it up, if not then you must take it up again. Remember you must give and repeat your verbal aid. In the end you should be able to ask him to pull and back up at the same time.

LESSON 5

HE IS GOING WELL, NOW HE WORKS FREE

This lesson has very little text because I feel the pictures are self-explanatory. Do study them and you will see how my body movements differ for the majority of exercises but the one thing they all have in common (which you cannot see) is that they are tied in with my voice aids.

Do not go into this phase of work with your horse until you have all of the exercises established on the lunge. Most important of all is that he must come to you when called, your voice is your braking system. So if he has a blank ask him to halt then either go out to him or bring him in. Have a good think about why there was a problem. As I have said before, if necessary go back two steps, put him back on the lunge or get a friend to help.

Whatever happens do not panic. Even if you find you cannot work your horse off the lunge just think what fun both of you will have while trying. Remember the reason you and your horse are together is because you are partners and friends.

Jack starts off on the left rein then changes across . . .

canters round then goes forward to halt . . .

he moves forward and round into a volte.

Jack now changes the rein . . .

forward to halt . . .

left leg lift . . .

followed by the start. . .

the middle. . .

and the completion of the pirouette.

Coming in followed by rein back and halt . . .

accepting the whips . . .

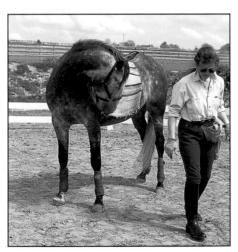 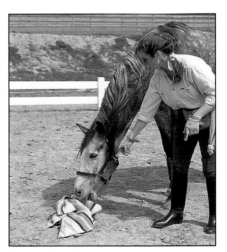

I put on his saddle blanket and go to get the saddle . . .

he takes if off, so I point and ask him to pick up . . .

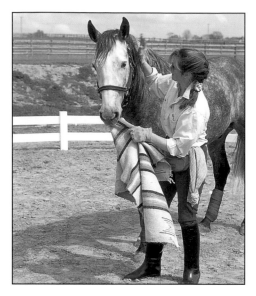

he responds and I praise him . . .

he then goes into a super stretch before . . .

he pushes me out . . .

finally he holds the whip while I open the gate and let us out.

LESSON 6

EDUCATING ANG STIMULATING—PROGRESSING INTO FREESTYLE

I think that we could almost call this lesson 'horse agility'. As I have mentioned earlier, we work on the basis that the more a horse learns from the floor the better it is for him in the long run. The good side to the voice training and the work from the ground is that it can be used for all ages of both horse and human.

One lady whom I had known for a long time from meeting her at shows had never seen our work until she came to one of our demonstrations. On returning home she went back to her eighteen-year-old horse and decided to work on the liberty and voice training. Next time I saw her she came up and said 'that stuff really works you know!' So there is hope for any age. Progressing to this stage will not only give you both confidence but I think will show you how much you and your horse understand each other, as well as preparing him for things he might meet on his travels in life.

Some of the things suggested you might feel have no purpose, however I believe that is where you are wrong. For me it is just plain fun, there does not always have to be a reason why.

For instance, I decided to take up the guitar and I went to night school but I could not understand why I was not finding it very easy, particularly as I have an ear for music, in as much as I do all the choreography for the displays. When I told my friends that my guitar and I could not agree where the notes should be, they laughed and said 'why bother, you do not need to play it'. Totally true but they missed the point, which is that I was enjoying trying and having fun. Have I mastered those notes yet? Well no, but I am still having fun!

At the time of writing we are building our 'Start for Life' arena and are including many of the things we already use and some new sections to work with. You can, though, do this next piece of work anywhere, it does not matter if you have not been able to cover the full liberty work because you do not have a round. It is important, however, that you cover the basics with your horse on the lunge and have taught him the words; this you can do in any area. Remember the most important words for your horse are his name, 'halt' and 'come here'.

If for any reason you do not feel happy letting your horse off the lunge, maybe the field is too big, give yourself another goal. Get your horse working on the end of the lunge line going

through the things I describe below. Work out a programme to suit yourself, hold the lunge about four feet (120cm) away from your horse, then as you both get the hang of it feed him further out. All the time give very clear voice aids and directions with your hand if needed. Remember practice and patience.

I feel this side of working with horses is only practised by the very few – there again I could be wrong. I think it would make rather a good handy-horse competition for people to do, just for fun. Before any work make sure your hip bag is full; do not give him food all the time as it can cause bad habits but always give him a treat at the end of work.

Sometimes I find that no matter how many times I say 'no, really don't do that because', to the person I am training it does seem that the request is not taken on board. As long as neither horse nor human can come to harm I will let nature take its course.

This actually happened when one of my 'legs' in the Mini Marvels[R] kept on giving her Mini a tasty treat every time he did something well or even when they halted. Her heart was in the right place but she was duly shown up by little Tom in the least appropriate place, in fact it was at our debut!

When working through the programme Tom had to stand still by the half-way marker, while his partner Warrior stood across the arena on the opposite side. Warrior stood like a little statue but suddenly Tom decided he had waited long enough without a treat. As his handler was so busy watching us and getting ready to move into her position with Tom, he caught her totally off guard when he simply turned around and stuck his nose in her pocket, refusing to move until he had been fed, much to the amusement of the audience!

THE START

Do wear gloves just as a precaution, leave a headcollar on and initially the lightest lunge you have. Walk around leading your horse and keeping him up level with your shoulder but in the region of four feet (120cm) away from you. If he tries to come in point to his shoulder and say 'no, out' giving praise as he responds. If he does not move out just flick the end of the lunge towards his shoulder, move towards him and at the same time repeat the verbal aids. Give much praise even if he only moves out a bit – it is a start.

ARENA PRACTICE

Leading your horse with a loose lunge, practise walking and halting around the edge of the arena. Try not to use the lunge as it is easy to become dependent on it, keep that as your emergency measure. Make sure that your horse is reacting to your voice aids. Walk as normal keeping your head up and only making eye contact when you want to. When you make a definite turn either right or left give him a verbal half halt first, maybe 'steady' and follow this with 'turn left' or 'turn right'. You can indicate with your hand left or right if you want but I feel it is better to try not to. Keep them as your emergency back-up. You do not have to use these words because, remember our horses learn to associate whatever words we teach them with the movements. A good idea is to incorporate other movements such as changes of rein through the diagonals, circles, loops, even serpentines. Always make sure that you keep the distance between you both. You should be able to work your horse from both sides, so do practise that.

From the halt Jack is coming towards me positively when called (I have moved back out of the picture).

HALT

As you are walking beside your horse make sure that when you ask for halt you stop your forward movement at the same time. Verbally ask him to 'halt' and 'stand', then move away. Keep hold of the lunge but do allow it to be loose while you move away, keep looking at him, this way he stays focused on you. If he makes to walk towards you lift your hand up and say 'no, halt', follow that up with praise when he responds. Walk back to him giving plenty of praise. Again, walk away, wait, then ask him to 'come here', step back a little as you did in the round, this way it is a very clear request.

Your horse has a wide range of vision so, when halting and standing, also practise walking back away from him, at the same time feeding out the lunge so it is very loose. Talk to him, repeat your verbal aids, increase the distance and the time away from him, even walk around and come back up the other side. If you do that make sure the lunge is well away from his feet. Do remember to keep talking to him and warn him when something is going to be done. Always give him plenty of praise whenever he has done what you have asked for.

REIN BACK

When he is settled at the halt bring him forward one step then ask for rein back, you can do this either standing by his shoulder or from the front facing him. When I do this work from the front

facing my horse, I walk very positively towards him at the same time telling him to go back. If there is a problem you can touch him with the end of the rope gently on the chest, the minute he responds give him plenty of praise.

To do this from the side, face the front and stand beside your horse's shoulder and tell him 'back' and at the same time you take a step backwards. If for any reason your horse does not move back when asked, place your hand closest to him on his chest and tap or feel the rope. As he responds to the pressure cease it but keep giving the verbal aid and praise him. Stop asking him to go back when you want him to stand still. I use the voice aid 'all right halt' and give praise.

If I find that the horse I am working with keeps going crooked when I am asking him to back up I find it helpful if I place some raised poles for him to back through. The poles must not move if they are touched otherwise this could unsettle him. First walk him forward through them so he sees where they are, then give him the aids for back. Just do a few steps to start and build them up as he gains confidence.

THE SLOW WALK

It is necessary to be able to ask your horse to walk slowly, particularly if you are to take him over unsteady ground or when approaching awkward obstacles.

Keeping four feet (120cm) away, hold the rolled-up lunge in your left hand, face the direction your horse is walking in and with the right hand also on the lunge use this to give a feel in conjunction with your voice aid so it would be 'listen, slowly'. You can also lift the left hand to the front at the same time, then drop it

as you say 'all right, walk on'. Remember to keep the tone of your voice soft and drawn out.

OBSTACLES

Normally you would not find this type of work in the liberty section, but I felt that as the work is done from the floor with a lunge, it should be covered and it is also extremely useful.

If you can, it is worth making things that your horse learns to negotiate by going over, on, under or through. This is the section that will help to prepare him for things that he might come across or that will just help him to understand how to cope with what he is being asked to do. For instance many people do not think about how the horse feels when he is put into a lorry or trailer particularly for the first time. Three things come to mind straight away: the sound is hollow, consequently the horse senses it is unstable, the partitions may restrict his balancing movement if they are placed too close together and very importantly the horse must lower his head to enter.

Obviously you can use anything, I have only given a few examples but I would suggest that you follow the same way of introducing your horse to them. Your horse can be of any age but if he is a youngster he does need to have done the basic work with you first, even if he is not yet being ridden.

STEPPING

I like my horse to be able to step over things without fuss. Stepping over a height is good for

the mobility of the muscles and joints. Start with two poles spaced apart on the ground (it does not matter if they are coloured). Keep a distance but walk parallel with your horse. Point with your hand, send him to the centre of the poles, praise him as he gets close and give a feel on the lunge and say 'listen, look'. As he goes to walk over say 'steady' or 'slowly'. You are wanting him to think about where his legs are so do not be tempted to keep a tight hold on him while he goes over the poles. If he hits the poles he will not do it again because he made the mistake that time, next time he will think. He should be able to lower his neck if needed as this helps him to balance and allows his hind leg to come higher.

Give him plenty of praise when he completes the exercise. Over a period of time lift the poles higher and as he builds up confidence bring them closer, then maybe add one or two more.

There are various thoughts on and even experiments to find out if horses can see colour. I cannot give scientific evidence but in my younger days we had a pony called Dandy who was great for the patience. One day I was trying to get him to walk over a coloured pole on the floor and I said to Mum as I went to the field that I wouldn't be long. He did not want to know and after an hour Mum came up to see where I was but I did not know she was watching. At that point I was standing on the floor explaining to him that the pole would not bite him. He still would not budge but interestingly he would go over a plain pole. I decided to sit it out, so I got back on and unbeknown to me my parents kept making spot checks to see what was happening. After standing there for three hours, I had eaten my snacks and was getting rather tired when suddenly for no rhyme or reason he just walked over the coloured pole.

THE BRIDGE

For getting horses used to the sound of hollow floors and for use in our Western trail work, we have a wooden bridge that comes about six inches (15cm) off the floor and is three feet (1m) wide. When starting over this put straw bales on each side to help guide your horse over. Lead him up to the bridge and give the verbal aid 'listen, look'. Encourage him to drop his head by feeling on the lunge in a downward motion and as soon as he gives, ease the pressure, then repeat until he puts the two requests together. Praise him, let him touch and sniff the bridge then ask him to walk on, at the same time feel on the lunge. If he does not come when asked, ease the pressure as he moves forward and use your voice to coax him on to it. Let him take his time and do not try to rush him, whatever progress he makes praise him. Some will go straight on, others debate and think about it, then very slowly go. If he keeps coming over to you then have someone on the offside with a lunge as this will help to keep him straight.

Keep talking to him saying 'steady' as he goes over the bridge and just give a feel on the lunge if he tries to rush. Once he gets used to the sound and the feel of the bridge ask him to stand still on it, make a big fuss when he does it and I would also give him a tasty treat for this. To get him used to the noise you could also walk him over a big piece of wood.

When we started the Minis walking over the bridge, all were fine except Boysie. The others had gone over the length of it but he did not want to know. He was not sure about it but the handler was even more worried, which then affected him. So I led him to the short side and put a lot of carrots on it, then he had Tom on one side and Bambi on the other to help give him

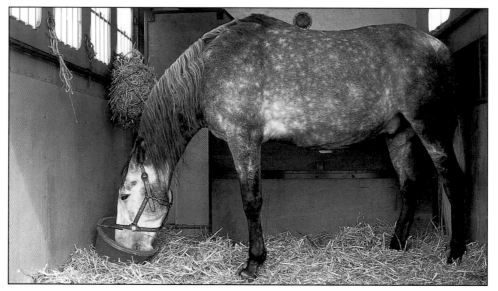

Having prepared Jack with the bridge and sounds he is quite happy to walk up the ramp on his own and, yes, there is a reward at the end of it.

confidence. I wanted him to do it by his own wish when he found that he could not evade the issue due to the positioning of the other two. His brother and sister were not bothered by the bridge so he started to feel confident and in the end he was leading the way.

We also use big plastic sheets, which can be off-putting to some. Jack walked straight on and started to play with it, whereas Vinnie could not cope. As I did not want to build this thing up into a big problem I resorted to food. Even when I stood on it he kept circling around me so I

placed a bucket of food just out of his reach, he leant in as far as possible without his feet coming onto the plastic and grabbed a bit of food. Then I moved it into the middle and he put two feet on and finally walked right over to get to the food on the other side. I then left him loose in the pen with the plastic and with food dropped all over it.

A SENSITIVE OR WORRIED HORSE

This is a horse that I would call spooky or sharp when introduced to new things, so we will put different items in the stable with him. Starting off with only one or two things, maybe paper bags which rustle but won't hurt him, we build up the items. It is the same for hanging things in the stable. Start off with a few items and as he gets used to them being there, add more. We will also hang string in the doorway so that he gets used to being touched at any time. If you do this be careful when leading your horse out of the stable – it would be safer to tie back any hanging objects.

With the number of horses that have made their way to us I have been made very aware that, just as there are many different types of personalities in people, so the same goes for horses. One who springs to mind is Hans who, despite all the work done at home and travelling to shows, gave me quite a reminder about not taking him for granted. We had been competing and doing very well all season, so I was rather confident at a final championship. Mistake, big time! Unfortunately the commentator gave us rather a big build up and inwardly I was saying 'please shut up'. To cut a long story short, as we trotted around the arena the flags were waving

Helping to desensitise the sensitive horse.

very strongly but we managed to cope with that. The bell went and we turned to enter at A then Hans saw the big colourful flower pots four feet away. He stopped dead, dropping his head down and spreading his front legs, rather like a startled giraffe. We managed to get into the arena but every time we reached that end there were fireworks. I knew at that point our marks were running rather low so to save the indignity of seeing them on the board I retired before the last movement! Hans is still a sensitive horse but the trust we have in each other is shown when I ride him with no saddle or bridle at my demonstrations. Mind you, I do ask the audience for no sudden movements as I canter past them.

GOING FREE

When you decide that you are going to work your horse free, do make sure that he is well exercised first! It makes sense that you are both in the right mental attitude to work. Run him through the basics with a lunge line on and once you are both confident take off the lunge. Obviously your horse must really be well onto your voice aids and able to focus on you as and when needed.

Make sure that your hip bag is full of goodies because if all else fails to bring your horse to you, I promise that bag will succeed. I have absolutely no qualms about using food as bribery!

If you can master all of the above without having to resort to bringing the lunge into effect then you are ready to work absolutely free. Do make sure that you are in a safe place when you take the

This is what you are aiming for. It is important to make sure your horse looks in the direction he is going and Jack is clearly doing so in both photographs.

lunge off your horse. Now, do go through all of the above work again but without the security of the lunge line, take your time and do not panic. If you have a problem ask your horse to halt, call him in, then start again. You can also do the obstacle work as well if you feel ready to have a go. Good luck.

PART 3

GET STARTED WITH LONG REINING

INTRODUCTION

I am surprised really that more people do not work their horses or ponies on two reins; possibly it is thought that you only do it with youngsters. We have found at our demonstrations that this form of work gets people talking and at the end of the lectures we now ask if anyone in the audience would like to have a go. Often we can have up to forty people of all ages wanting to try. Many did not realise that you can actually do it whatever the size or age of your horse.

During one lesson I asked a rider how often they worked or exercised their horse on a lunge or long reins. She said to me 'Why should I bother? I ride my horse everyday'. If you had seen the horse you would understand why I asked the question. When being ridden he was hollow and not accepting the bit or the contact. Consequently life was being made very uncomfortable for this horse and he could, in time, develop physical problems. I think it is useful and helpful to watch a horse working but without the weight of the rider on his back. This way you can see exactly what is happening to his muscles, whether he is holding himself in a certain manner and the length of stride he is taking. Not everyone can feel what is happening underneath, it is actually possible to get so used

to a way of going, that it does feel correct and comfortable but in fact there is a problem.

As a re-schooling aid I find lungeing and long reining invaluable. An interesting thing has been occurring in the last few years and this is that I have been approached by vets to assist with horses to see if a problem was medical or rider induced. Personally I think that these vets are forward thinking which can only be for the good of the horse. A lot of vets do not ride and sometimes what the rider is feeling cannot be seen from the floor. On the other hand it may be that the vet cannot find any medical reason for the way the horse is going or behaving. This is because the rider is the cause of the problem in either their riding or horse management. This is where we come in – by having a different rider and different management structure for a week or two I can help analyse the problems. Before we do anything I will see the horse and his owner at home, see him being ridden and handled in the stable and enquire about his feeding and living arrangements. All these parts help to build up the whole picture.

When the horse comes to us I do not ride him for the first few days but I will introduce him first to the lunge. At these times I do not have an assistant because I want to see exactly how the

Here are two reiners from one of our days having their first ever long-reining session. Cobby and Pinza only have blinkers (closed bridles) on due to shortage of open (no blinkers) working bridles.

horse will behave. This gives him a chance not only to focus but he also learns to listen to me. In turn this gives me the time to study him and from the lunge I move on to two reins on the circle, where I do a lot of transitional and stretching work.

One horse arrived with very tight muscles in the hindquarters. They tightened up and looked like apples each side of the spine when the saddle went on and stayed that way whilst he was being exercised. It would be easy to assume he had a physical problem so it was important to see how he reacted to our working process. Also

he was not carrying the sort of condition that I would expect, either in muscular development or just body-covering meat. Following a few days of being lunged, then long reined combined with turning him out to allow the physical freedom and the mental relaxation he desperately needed, the tension did go even when he was ridden. It appeared that his owner would not let him go free in case he hurt himself, so when he got wound up his food was cut down to the lowest rations and kept down. Unfortunately for this horse they had neither the right attitude nor facilities, in fact they had

The Mini Marvels^R just finishing their performance at the Sandringham Driving Championship and Country Fair. (Left to right), Gladiator, Goliath, Warrior, Samson, Spartacus and Hercules.

the problem not the horse. He went home after being handled and ridden by his owner while with us and I only hope they had the courage to change their ways. We can only offer advice.

All my horses are worked either on the lunge or long reined. I am sure that you have had a day when, whatever the reason, you did not feel like riding. I certainly have and at these times I will lunge purely to stretch the horse's legs using a lunge and a headcollar or bridle. If I want to work him from the floor then I will lunge him with side-reins or work with two reins on the circle.

I always long rein our youngstock before we start to ride them, this will follow on from their being confident and safe on the lunge. Also they have a good understanding of the basic word range so, if there is a problem, we can say the name, 'come here' or 'halt'. By doing this work

they are also building and strengthening their muscles, particularly over the back before carrying weight. They will be mouthed and able to do basic work. Another useful aspect of using two reins on the circle is that it does keep control of the hindquarters. This is quite a common pro-blem when lungeing, particularly if the horse is stiff. He will literally swing the quarters out, so he no longer moves on the single track but on two which is incorrect, unless you are asking for it! Everything you do with your horse is designed to make life easier for you both. Remember if there is a problem and the reason is not obvious, analyse it before anything else is done.

LESSON 7

SAFETY FIRST

SAFETY FOR YOU AND YOUR HORSE

It really is vitally important that both you and your horse are totally conversant with lungeing. Not everyone will want to do the liberty work, that's fine, but your horse should be well trained to the voice aids, listening to you and doing basic lunge work. When we start our horses we hang pieces of equipment from the saddle and this way they get used to all sorts of sensations before lunges go around them. I would also do this with a horse who is shy, sharp or ticklish because this way he becomes desensitised to possible irritants. Only then when you are happy with your horse's attitude should you progress to long reining.

I feel one has to be sensible about where to start this work, it would be very unfair to your horse and difficult for you if it was decided to try it in the field. You need to make sure that the area is such that if he gets a fright or you have a problem with the lunges neither of you is in danger even if he gets loose. I would advise that you should go for an enclosed area.

As with all the work in this book, make sure that there are not any distractions around when you begin working. It is in both your interests that you can concentrate on each other. You will progress onto obstacles when you are ready. Do wear a hat and gloves when doing this work.

ASSISTANCE

No matter what age or how good your horse is when he is on the lunge, you must not take it for granted that he will be the same when you first put on the second lunge. It is really imperative that someone is with you for the first few times in case you need a hand.

LESSON 8

TACK AND ITS CORRECT FITTING

ON YOUR HORSE'S HEAD

You can use a normal snaffle bridle, a close-fitting headcollar or a lunge cavesson which has rings each side. Personally I always use a bridle for this work as I feel that it is an important safety aspect. Do take your horse's age into account as he may be teething, consequently his mouth will be very uncomfortable, so in this instance I would not use a bridle.

THE SADDLE AND THE ROLLER

You can use either a saddle or roller. I have used a saddle in my pictures as I felt that the majority of readers would have one to hand. The stirrups need to be secured down and we do this by using one side rein, or similar, connected to the offside stirrup and bringing it under the belly lying on top of the girth. Connect it to the nearside stirrup making sure that it is tight enough to stop any movement when the reins are in place. On the whole I put the reins level with the bottom of the flap of the saddle.

If you decide to long rein on a regular basis you might find a roller handy and for ease have one that unbuckles both sides. They are available in a variety of materials. Make sure it is big enough to fit over the saddle in case you wish to work before you ride. I have had rings put on ours in different places, this way I can work in whatever mode I wish from just stretching and loosening on the lower to middle rings, to moving up higher for the advanced level.

THE LUNGE REINS

Depending on the size of horse or pony you are long reining, the length will vary from nine to twenty-four feet (2.8 to 7.4m). Do make sure that they are separate reins. You can use whatever is the most comfortable in your hands, from leather to webbing. I like to use ones that are a good weight in the hand, this way if I tap the horse on the side he can feel it.

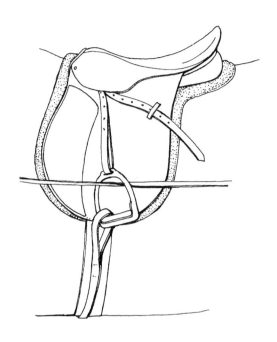

Stirrup connection under belly.

THE WHIP

It is up to you whether or not you carry a whip, depending on your horse's attitude and if he goes forward willingly.

LEG PROTECTION

If it is a young horse that I am starting in this work or one that might be sharp and could possibly bang his legs, then I would put on either boots or bandages but I must admit it is not something that I do as a matter of course. Some horses with very sensitive skin do not like having things on their legs, getting upset because they get hot and sweaty.

LESSON 9

FROM ONE TO TWO REINS

THE LUNGE REIN

It is imperative that you and your horse are confident and have the basic lunge work well confirmed. Before moving on I would also lunge him with a long blanket that has a fillet string attached so he will feel this on his legs when moving. Place this under the saddle or the roller. This gets your horse used to movement around his body while he is working.

Long reining is the next logical step on from the single lunge rein. Do make sure that your horse is relaxed. Give him a rub all over with your hands, let the lunges bang and touch him and keep talking so that he knows by your voice everything is in order.

GOING TO TWO REINS

Start on the left rein with your helper on the outside, who can put a lead rope through the bit. Make sure that you have asked your horse to stand while you are organising lunges. It is debatable whether or not one should put the lunges straight through the stirrups if you have not done this work before. However, when I am teaching people they seem to have less problems when the outside lunge is held up by the stirrup, possibly it is because they are not having to worry about not only keeping the horse going but also making sure they do not drop the lunges down round the horse's legs and creating a problem.

I would suggest that the inside lunge is placed onto the bit coming to your hand as if lungeing. Place the outside one over the saddle getting your helper to put it through the stirrup and connect it to the bit. Make sure that the outside lunge does not slip off thereby getting caught between the saddle and the horse's back, and causing friction burn. Give you horse plenty of praise all the time you are working around him.

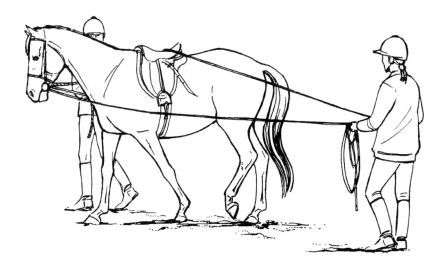

Getting started on two reins.

LESSON 10

PRELIMINARY WORK
WITH TWO REINS

YOUR POSITION

It is very important that there is no tension in the upper body, make a conscious effort to feel what your muscles are doing, are they tight or relaxed? Some of the most common problems are in the shoulders, elbows and the hands. A good exercise is to actually tighten each set of muscles individually then release them, having the ability to do this will give you more body awareness and control. You will long rein in the manner you ride, so beware. Ideally you should stand tall without tension, your elbows by your sides or just in front of the body, they must not be stiff. Follow your horse but do not pull back on his mouth.

When I have my Mini Marvels[R] practising, each person watches the one in front. I have noticed that particularly when going into the two-track exercises or when teaching the horse new movements it is very common for the handlers to start dropping a shoulder, tipping their heads, even lifting a hand. If they do not make their own correction, someone will say 'what are you doing?' That is normally all that needs to be said.

All bad habits are best caught at the beginning – it can be very easy when working on your own to develop bad ones. When I am working with anyone I will ask them 'what are you feeling, what is happening, why are you doing that?' These are not trick questions but they make the person think about what they are doing and if necessary ask me questions. It is all about thinking riding or thinking work, whichever, it will also apply to you. Do not think only of the horse, you must be aware of what you are doing. How are your arms? Are they tense? Is your back solid? Are your hands hanging onto the reins? Is your bottom underneath you or are you losing your balance?

Whatever you do will either directly or indirectly affect how your horse will proceed, just the same as when riding.

On the circle even though you have two reins, as with lungeing you must be careful not to get in front of your horse's eyeline, otherwise this might cause him to stop. If this happens do not panic or chastise him, simply sort yourself out and ask him to walk on. Remember it does take time to learn these things, if it didn't then trainers and authors would be out of a job!

This shows well the position of the lunge over the saddle and Louise's position by Jack's shoulder.

REIN CONTACT

You want him to take both the reins equally: the inside rein asks for flexion and the outside one controls the bend. When he moves off, allow him to go. You need to give your horse a confident, steady feel on the reins. Be careful not to have one or both reins loose, if that happens quickly take them up. Do not hold them like pieces of glass, you need to be able to talk down the reins with your hands. In return your horse should take the bit but not lean on it. If he does then you need to give him a half halt with the reins and the voice aid 'listen up', at the same time a little touch on the hock should help to get him to carry himself.

THE MOVE OFF

Following the previous procedure for where to put the lunges (the inside one direct to your hand and the outside one through the stirrup over the saddle to your hand) you are now ready for the move off. Standing at your horse's shoulder you are going to work on him on a circle to begin with. If you have done your preparation properly life will be so much easier.

You can do this in two ways. The first is to ask your horse to stand on the track of the circle, the helper by his shoulder on the outside ready to follow and help if needed. Keep looking and talking to the horse while you feed out the lunges as you move back towards the centre of the circle. Say his name followed by 'listen and walk on'. Get the feel of what it is like if you have not done this before, you will need to walk

a good-sized circle to start with while your horse is using the full distance of the circle around you. As you both become at ease with this way of working, the lunges lengthen so that you are now turning in a small area. Your helper should walk on the outside.

The other way to move off is to be in the centre of the circle with a lunge in each hand. You stand by his shoulder facing him. Get his attention by saying his name followed by 'listen and walk on', send him off with your inside hand, feed the lunges out through your hands as he goes towards the track. As he approaches it feel on the inside lunge and tell him to 'turn left'. As this is happening make sure that your outside lunge is letting him complete the request. Your helper will lead him out if he is not sure. The aim is to get him walking around you with no fuss and accepting the two reins. The closer you are the more control you will have but I prefer to get my horses well out and away from me to start. Use lots of voice praise; if he gets worried just feel down the reins, a form of half halt, and tell him to 'steady'.

POSSIBLE PROBLEM, AND CORRECTION, OF FALLING-OUT

Be careful not to use too much inside rein because this can cause your horse to bend too much in the neck and create a problem of him falling-out through the shoulder. In other words you will try to bring him around but only the head and neck goes where you want and the rest of the body goes sideways. Even if you try to make a correction with the outside rein it can be difficult – some horses realise this can be fun and they keep doing it!

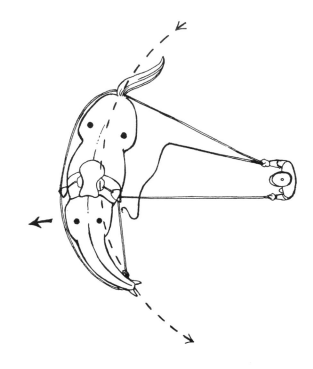

Because of the whip position and too much inside rein you can see how the shoulders have fallen out and off the centre line, note the placing of the front feet.

If a horse is tender on one side of the mouth, when he is asked to give more flexion or come closer, the bit hurts him, so he might evade in this way. He takes action to get away from the pain, some will even rear up to get away from it. A lot depends on what has happened to the horse in the past and how he was ridden. He may have lost confidence in any contact to his mouth and you will not always know the cause of the problem. I hope you do not meet these problems because horses like this should really have an experienced person to help them gain their confidence.

If your horse falls-out you need to ask him to halt, feel down the reins and use your voice.

When he responds walk up to him taking up your reins and get sorted out. Stay close to his shoulders, place your hands up by the withers and hold the reins as if you were riding, then squeeze the outside rein and ask him to bend to the outside. When he does, give him plenty of praise and slowly straighten his neck again with the inside rein. Practise this a couple of times, also bend him to the inside and straighten. By doing this you are giving him time to understand your requests. It will also make you aware of how much pressure is needed to show your horse what you want him to do. Maybe you are giving too strong an aid with one hand which is creating the problem.

Staying in the same position, ask him to walk on and as you are close you should now find it easier to control your horse's shoulder. Remember he moves from the back end first, so depending on your hands they will either allow him to move 'through' you or they will 'block' him. Think of this when you are working, it is really important to all the work, ridden or in-hand.

As you get more confident and can control his shoulders and work him on the reins without him falling-out then slowly ease him on to a bigger circle. Do not drop the inside contact in order to direct him out but allow him to follow where the outside lunge is asking him to go. There should not be any neck swinging, just following where his nose takes him.

POSSIBLE PROBLEM, AND CORRECTION, OF FALLING-IN

The opposite of falling-out is falling-in. Your horse is on the circle but has a wrong bend and is looking out. The horse's weight goes into the inside shoulder so he loses balance, consequently he will come in closer or fall-in to you. Just using the outside rein to try and direct him out will not help, it will simply exaggerate the problem. If you are experienced, the way to correct this would be to shorten the inside rein and, giving a positive feel on it, bring him onto a smaller circle. I would keep asking him to flex in and to do this he needs to let go of the bit on the inside and take the outside rein equally, this is normally the cause of the problem in an older horse. While I am working him on the smaller circle I would touch him on the shoulder with the whip and say 'out', followed up with a touch on the hock and I would tell him 'forwards' because this makes sure we keep up the activity. All the time I would be feeling with the inside rein and allowing with the outside and encouraging him to work around me with the right flexion and contact. Falling-in can also happen because he is unbalanced, does not understand or he could be stiff. Maybe you have not started him off correctly going into equal contact but are using only the outside rein to direct him out.

The easiest way for you to correct this would be to bring him to halt: use your voice, feel down both reins and step in front of his eyeline, remember you did this in the lunge work. Walk towards him, taking the reins up at the same time and talk to him, he might be worried. Standing next to him, squeeze the inside rein and ask him to relax his jaw, do not drop the outside contact but allow him to bend and follow the asking rein. Do this a few times so that he understands what you are asking. Give plenty of praise however small the response. You are only looking for him to flex to the inside not to bend as in a stretching exercise. While he is

responding, touch him with your fingers on the girth area and ask him to move away from the pressure. This shows him that you are wanting him to move around you with the correct bend. All the time give lots of voice encouragement.

To progress this onto the circle I would have the helper on the inside, this way they do not counteract your inside rein. Let him move onto a small circle but still flexing to the correct direction. If you have a helper you should not need the lunge whip as they can touch him in the girth area. If you do not have a helper use the lunge whip and touch your horse on the shoulder or the girth area, at the same time giving the verbal aid 'out' then praise him as he responds. Make sure that you feel on the inside rein to get your horse looking in the right direction at the same time and allow the new bend through with your outside rein.

This should help correct the problem but it can take time for him to understand and for you to get not only the coordination but the ability to anticipate things before they happen so that you can preempt the problem before it happens. It might sound complicated but patience, time and practice will make these manoeuvres manageable. I have included these two problems early on because they are very common even at the starting stages.

THE HALT

The main difference with halting on the two reins compared to when lungeing the horse is that you should not move from your position. Give your horse the aid 'listen and halt' and at the same time give equal pressure on both reins. Be careful not to release your aid too quickly or

he may think it was just a half halt.

One horse I prepared for the show ring had a slightly hot temperament and he would get worked up when he had to stand still. So to start with I would ask him to stand, using my voice and keeping a contact on the reins so that when he went to move forward I gave a feel down them and said 'good boy halt' easing off the minute he responded. By slowly increasing the time spent standing, making much of him with praise and yes, giving him food, it helped to break the anxiety he was having. We also walked lots of other horses around as if in a ring and when he could cope with that they started to change the pace. I just kept making much of him.

CHANGE OF DIRECTION

As you and your horse become comfortable with going round, practise asking him to halt and walk on. Keeping your helper on the outside, call your horse's name to get his attention, then ask him verbally to halt and at the same time feel down the reins. I like to keep everything equal because it is easy to be a little stronger on one rein without realising it, which can then create a problem. When he responds give plenty of praise, then ask him to walk on again.

When he has halted and you are happy that he is listening, walk up to him making sure you take up the reins as you go, then lead him into the middle. You will need to change the lunges so that your new outside one will go through the stirrup and the new inside one direct to your hand. Your helper now needs to change sides, again you need to touch your horse with the lunges all over the quarters and around the legs.

I cannot stress enough that you must not take your horse for granted when working with the two reins or when touching him around the quarters. So with a lunge in each hand, staying close and touching him whilst you are talking to him bring the lunge into the new positions. When you are ready then proceed to move off again, practising the walking and halting.

Starting the change from the right-rein circle to the left, I ease the inside rein and ask with the outside rein for the new flexion.

Jack is now looking to the new direction.

He has completed the change but is a little behind the bit — you can see his nose is just behind the vertical.

LESSON 11

PROGRESSING WITH TWO-REIN WORK ON THE CIRCLE

Do not rush any of the work in the previous lesson. You horse should be happy to walk and halt when asked and come into the centre to change direction. At this point your outside rein is still coming over his back. As with everything, if the basics are not established you will not have a stepping stone to go back to if there is a problem. There is not a time limit for any work you do, it is not a race.

Your horse should now be ready to move on and take the outside rein around the quarters. Stand him in the middle of the circle, with your assistant on the outside. Making sure the outside lunge is through the stirrup, let it slip down over the quarters, the inside one is still direct to your hand. Give your horse praise, get his attention then ask him to 'walk on'. When he moves off try to feel the rhythm of the outside lunge against the quarters, you need to allow this movement to happen – do not try to stop it. If you are carrying a whip you might find it easier to hold it in the inside lunge-rein hand, pointing underneath the second rein towards the back end. This might take some practice. Keeping the inside lunge directly to your hand at this stage will make it much easier to bring your horse into

you if he panics with the outside lunge around his quarters.

TRANSITIONS

Transitions are the changes either from one pace to another or within the paces such as collected to working, they are valuable for encouraging the horse to engage his hind legs, get him listening to you and lightening the forehand.

If your horse is happy with the lunge around his quarters doing the transitions on both reins I would now put the inside lunge through the stirrup. When you have done this send your horse out onto the circle holding the lunges as before. You will most probably get a different feel from your horse because of the angle of the lunge from the bit to the stirrup then to your hand. When he is going round watch out that you do not get in front of him as this will put more pressure on the inside lunge, possibly creating a problem. Remember to warn him with the half halt and the verbal aid 'listen' before you ask him to do something and think about the

tone that you are using. You will now also be able to change your horse's direction without stopping to change the lunge position. To keep this movement flowing through, remember that during the stride your horse takes while changing direction you must shorten your new inside lunge and lengthen the new outside one. This is how you will go through the movement on the left rein. Remember you are wanting your horse to change through the centre of the circle. Feel the inside rein, tell him, 'steady, change', allow him to follow the direction with your outside rein. You will need to be stepping away from the centre and as he goes through the centre start to feel on the new inside rein to show him the way. At this point you should be moving across behind at a safe distance. Keep talking to him, shorten the new inside rein and lengthen the outside one. Make sure you are now standing in the centre again. Praise him when the exercise is done.

CANTER TRANSITIONS

Really you should only progress to canter when your horse is able to do all the work in this section happily in walk and trot without any problem; this will show you that he is balanced and listening to you.

It is important when you are asking for the transition from trot to canter that you avoid two easy pitfalls. The first one being that your horse runs, in other words trots faster and falls into canter. Or, in the second case, in an effort to make sure he does not run you have him going so slowly that he does not have enough energy to strike off into canter. We have established that you have to hit the happy medium and have enough controlled energy for the strike-off. Working on the two lunges on the circle, make sure he is going equally into both reins, get a flexion to the inside by feeling down the rein. Do not overprepare, within a couple of strides warn him with 'listen, canter left'. In the beginning I also tend to tap them with the outside lunge rein at the same time as I give the verbal aid, this makes the request very clear. Make sure that you follow the movement and allow him to canter through your hands, do not stop him by blocking him. For the downward transitions feel on both reins and give him the verbal aid 'listen and trot', praise him when he responds. Practise this on both reins so that you can get either strike-off when you ask for it.

LESSON 12

WHERE TO STAND FOR LONG REINING

Before you move onto going large and long reining, a word about your position in relation to the horse's hind legs. I think that there are only two places you can be to work your horse. I will not say that any position is safe because I feel that one should always be aware of the element of risk involved when you are with horses, be it working, handling on the ground or riding. Freak accidents can happen and I lost a friend in a tragic one when there was no blame on either side. She was riding her horse in the indoor school and at the end of an extended canter on the diagonal by the wall the horse had a fatal heart attack and she was trapped underneath it.

Working on short reins close up to the quarters does give greater control for the more advanced work but I would only use this on a horse with whom I had done a lot of work on the long reins. If he kicks back for any reason you should not get the full brunt of the kick as you are so close, at least that is the theory.

I cannot give a 'dangerous' distance because this depends on your horse's height and the length of his hind leg! Do think carefully about where you position yourself because it could be that if he kicked back and you received the full force of impact it could be disfiguring or at the worst fatal. At a demonstration a gentleman with a badly disfigured lower jaw came up to me during the interval and said 'I am pleased you stressed where you should not stand, this is what happened to me when my youngster panicked'.

The safest place to long rein is well out of reach of the hind legs, it does seem rather strange to have the horse so far away from you but you will get used to it.

LESSON 13

GOING LARGE ON THE LONG REINS

PROGRESSING

When you can do all that has been mentioned in the previous lessons and your horse is accepting everything quietly and calmly, you are not getting tangled up or worried by the handling of the lunges then I would feel that you are both ready to progress to long reining at large.

I still keep the level of the stirrups at flap length as this helps to control the quarters. If you have them too high, a common problem is that the horse literally turns underneath the reins and ends up looking at you, this happens particularly to novice reiners. This cannot happen with the reins lower round the quarters and it also does away with the possibility of the lunge getting caught up underneath your horse's tail when working on the circle.

Sometimes it is possible that even when you have positioned everything correctly on your horse they will do a movement that will create a difficult situation. When Snowy went back to work after her return from racing and subsequent lay-off due to injury I started her off again on the horse walker. I then lunged and long reined her on the circle. One day I was long reining her and

she was very fresh and on her toes when suddenly she lowered her quarters and the lunge went under her tail which she then clamped down on it. This was a rather tricky problem with her back legs becoming very active. Even though she had done all the preparation work, you have to remember that horses are not machines and there will be hiccups. In this case I talked to her calmly and took up the reins, I let the outside one go and brought her into me. You may have to make an instant decision whether to bring the horse in or send him on round to see if he will settle down.

GOING LARGE ON LONG REINS

Working your horse in a circle on the two reins at the walk, get his attention by saying 'listen' then ask him to halt. When he has responded give him plenty of praise. Take up the outside lunge and walk out onto the track behind him, the lunges should be level. Keep talking so that he is aware that you are going to a different spot. The first time you are behind him, it would

Jack is showing good strides here at the trot and taking the bit. Notice the difference between his head position from the previous picture. He is now ready to go large.

be sensible to have your helper at your horse's head.

Before moving off you need to get his attention, say his name so that he does not get a surprise, give him the verbal aid 'listen, walk on left'. If you find he does not respond to the 'walk on' aid, repeat it and at the same time lightly tap him with the lunge on the quarters. Be sure to allow him through your hands and arms. Think about how you are feeling in your body, particularly if this is the first time you have done it. Is there any tension anywhere? If the answer is yes, then isolate it, remember to breathe, and let those muscles go. Your horse will read how you are so give clear, confident, verbal aids and have him walking well into the reins. My philosophy has always been: whatever you do, be positive.

BASIC EXERCISES

Practise the walk, halt, walk transitions when you first go large. The halt is very important and

if there is a problem your horse must halt the minute you ask and then wait for your next request. The voice is my primary aid and I like to have all my horses going into the reins equally, it is important to keep your horse straight through the transitions, particularly the downward ones. I use my voice aids and a feel on both reins to do them – be aware of how your hands are feeling on the reins.

You can take your horse onto a large circle making sure you start it and arrive back at the track at the same point. On returning to the track from the large circle put in a smaller one, I give one word for the movements I do. So to let your horse go onto the smaller circle give a verbal warning 'steady' followed by 'circle'. At the same time, but without pulling back, just feel on the inside rein, allow him to follow the direction he is being given but do not throw the contact away with the outside hand, you must keep a steady contact. Everything that you do with your horse should be subtle. As you are about to finish the movement think of going straight onto the track. You need to stop feeling down the inside rein and make sure you have the equal pressure again and tell him 'go straight'. Give plenty of praise when the movement is completed.

You might think it strange to tell your horse words for what you want him to do even in this work, considering that you have the reins to help you. All that I can say is that I talk to all my horses, the ridden ones included, even when I am competing. I have become a pretty good ventriloquist! Seriously though, the words are even more important if you are going to start to drive your horse.

Move on to the change of rein through the circle, which you can do by going straight across from where you turn off the track. Give the verbal warning 'steady' followed by 'turn left', if there is the time and space tell him 'go straight'. Once you have completed the first turn remember to stop asking for it, keep the feel down the reins equal. Do start to prepare for the next turn in good time, your horse's head is at least ten feet (3m) ahead of you, so if you are mentally behind him you will miss the 'turning point' when you could have given the aids. As with everything, practice will help you to prepare and follow through. You could also change through two half circles, the principle is the same. Give the verbal aid and at the same time ask with the inside rein. You might need to keep asking on the inside rein until the half circle is nearly finished, about two strides from the centre where the second half starts then you need to prepare your horse for the new direction. So stop asking with the inner rein, make sure he is straight and taking both reins equally before you start to feel on the new inside rein. If he does not answer give a little tap with the outside lunge and repeat the verbal aid. As time progresses you will not need to keep giving the aid because you will learn to set your horse up and he will start to learn what you are asking for and he will listen to you.

Finally you can change the rein when working your horse on two reins on the circle by turning him out on a small half circle thereby changing the rein and taking the new direction, as long as there is nothing to hinder him turning. When you are standing in the centre with him walking round on the left rein fix a spot with your eye where you will change direction when your horse's nose reaches it. As he approaches the spot give him the warning 'listen' then start to feel on the outside rein so that he flexes to the outside, you will need to step a few paces towards your horse as you let him follow the

I have asked Jack to work large but I would say that I am just in the 'safe area' for long reining. In fact, I could be about another foot or two further back, so be careful as you are not always as far back as you may think.

new bend to start the circle. At the same time give him the verbal aid 'circle right'. In order to allow him to do the half circle you must either shorten the new inside rein as he completes the movement or lengthen the new outside rein. You can do this by allowing your arm to go forward or by bending your arm more.

You can also make your horse walk in a serpentine up the centre line. For the serpentine you would actually start walking on the centre line but you would direct your horse across in front of you and he would do a series of half circles. This movement is not complicated but you do have to be well ahead of your horse and know at which point you are going to ask for the changes of direction.

When you are working large and following your horse make sure that you stay directly on the track behind him, it can be very easy to step in and go on a different track when your horse is turning or circling. Another habit that seems quite common with newcomers is that they more their hands away in order to turn, almost as if they are driving a wheelbarrow, it does not work. Trust me.

A little tip if you keep taking your hands apart is to carry a short piece of rope between your hands. This in turn should then give you the correct feel for the distance needed between the reins.

LESSON 14

USEFUL EXERCISES ON THE FLAT

SOME ADVICE

You should by now have mastered the basic exercises on the large circle and be incorporating them into the work you are doing when working at large. Not only can you do all the ridden movements when long reining but as you both become more competent you can stretch the range to include such things as going over banks, trotting poles and pairing up with a friend to make long reining pairs. This is particularly good for those of you who are too big to ride a pony or maybe cannot ride.

PROGRAMME PLANNING

When you start this or, in fact, any work it is easy to wander around aimlessly just circling, then when you finish you can be tired but you have not necessarily worked or even exercised your horse. It is worth planning the programme before you go out to start each session, do not stick to it rigidly but use it as a way of focusing on doing constructive building-block work. In the beginning it is worth taking a precautionary step back when you take up the reins for the next session, this just reiterates the previous lesson in both your minds. Obviously as you progress you will become more confident and do more thinking reining, so you should not need to keep doing this.

COPING WITH PROBLEMS

If for any reason you get into a problem that you just cannot see the way out of, bring your horse to the halt and then ask him to do something that you both find easy. Make a fuss of him, then put him away on a good note, you might think that by doing this the horse has 'won'. Never view training your horse as a win or lose scenario, if you do, then something is very wrong with your attitude and you need to have a good think about how the problem came about. Normally it is the reiner who has directed the horse incorrectly and given confusing aids, so the horse will get upset and worried when he cannot do what is being asked. If you can, have a

helper come and assist you on the next session so that your horse can be led through the trouble spot. If not, see if you can get something on video. This would then show you why there is trouble and by studying it you should be able to rectify it in your mind, then help your horse. It is better for the horse mentally and physically to do two shorter working sessions than one long one, especially if he is learning a new movement.

Despite all the preparatory work that we do with our horses and other animals to try to make life and situations easier to cope with, in the end I do not think that we can totally simulate real life experiences for them. So I always say to people, never take your horse for granted, particularly a young horse. This came to the fore one day when one of the girls was long reining the young horse Boysie. It had been raining so there was water lying on the arena. After settling him on the lunge, off they went on the long reins. Suddenly one of the dogs leapt up over the bank and gave him a fright. He jumped forward catching the handler off balance and she ended up taking enormous strides to keep up with him. The problem was that all that he could hear was a lot of noise behind which was frightening him. At that point we all walked in and she managed to steer him towards us which stopped him. A very lucky escape. I said that if that happened again then she should very quickly drop one rein and keep talking to the horse. At the same time she should bring him in by shortening the rein she was holding which is made easier by the fact that his neck is bent towards you. If you get in real trouble it is safer to let go, but you have to make an instant decision.

EXPANDING THE EXERCISES

The basic ones you have already practised – circles, changing rein and transitions – lead you on to doing the school figures – serpentines, diagonal changes of rein, turning across the school to change direction, figure of eight, half circle with diagonal line back to the track and centre lines. I do not need to repeat the aids because we went through them in the previous lesson, sometimes it can be helpful to talk yourself through the aids while doing movements.

Do not forget to go on straight lines and make sure that your horse is going forward positively into both reins. If he feels a little wobbly or is snaking (you will know what I mean if you meet it) tell him 'forwards' and tap him on the quarters

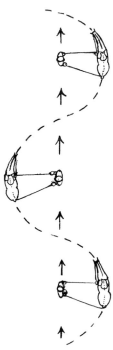

When doing the serpentine make sure you walk with your horse as shown, to keep the movement fluid and flowing.

Going sideways is not a problem — make sure you can go straight. Even on circles we practise keeping the horses straight as opposed to always asking for a bend.

with both reins, follow this with praise as he goes. This does happen sometimes when the horse is learning lateral work and starts to anticipate it, you should say 'no, forwards – good boy' then do some quick transitions with not many strides between each one. This should help get him straight and into the reins. Going sideways is not a problem, going straight can be!

For those of you who have not previously worked through any of the exercises, by having done the preparation work explained in the earlier lessons I am sure that you and your horse should now find it easier to have a go.

STARTING CAVALLETTI WORK AND POLE WORK

I find that working horses over cavalletti is useful for helping to improve the trot, the flexion of the joints and strengthening the hindquarters and it does encourage them to stretch over the top line. When placing them down the long side or on a circle, start with two cavalletti building up to between four and six. Set the distances within your horse's stride and as he starts to work comfortably open them up a little. Having them on the circle is good as you can start on the inner

ring, then ease him out over the wider distance. Do this by feeling the outside rein and allowing with the inside one, at the same time telling him 'out'.

When long reining over cavalletti either have the lunges in the positions that you have been working in or take them up higher bringing the outside lunge rein over your horse's back and to you. I often put poles of all colours down on the floor, not in measured or related distances and at different angles to each other. I want my horse to look at them and think about what his feet are doing. I have no wish to teach him to lift his legs, he needs to do that himself. By having the poles set down in this manner as well as having them at different heights he has to use his brain and flex his joints, both of which are beneficial to him. On reading through the other lessons I am sure that you may find you can include some of these exercises into your programme.

LESSON 15

INTRODUCING LATERAL WORK

LATERAL WORK

If you have covered the section 'can your horse bend, will he move away from pressure?' in Part 1 and gone through the process of showing your horse how to move away from pressure then you are ready to proceed with this work. If not, then go and get practising. It does not pay to try short cuts! With most of the movements I have only used inside or outside instead of left or right as it is easier and less confusing I think, particularly if like me you get these two mixed up! I have often told someone to go left yet pointed to the right! Anyway, if you are on a straight line but not in an arena, place yourself by anything such as a fence or tree line and call that your outside.

I hope that you have given your horse the words for the movements he has learnt from the floor, if not then put in some extra time and do it. You should be able to move his shoulder over while the quarters stay fairly stationary, this will lead into turn on the haunches then the walk pirouette. You can also practise keeping his shoulders as stationary as possible but moving the quarters around and this will take you into turn on the forehand.

To have the horse move away from pressure with all his body going sideways is full pass and will lead into passade (a very large walk piroutte) and half pass. Some people think of this as 'dressage' and therefore alien, but for me it is basic loosening up and gymnastic work which all horses should learn. It is good for his body, making him more supple and responsive, which makes him a nicer ride and it makes him use his brain. It is good fun, bringing you both onto another level of work and understanding of each other. Remember, I have not promised that it will always be easy, there might be the odd hiccup.

I cannot emphasise enough the need to use your voice and to know the words you will be using for all movements. Pronounce the words clearly, drawing them out so that they are not short and sharp. Keep the tone down, not a high pitched shrill. If your horse is not listening to the words then make the tone stronger. With all long-reining work establish it in the walk on both reins. Only progress to trot when you and your horse are happy and able to maintain what is being asked for over a good distance. Remember to keep breathing – you are now starting your fittening work!

TURN ON THE FOREHAND

For this movement your horse can either pivot on, or mark time with, his front legs while he moves his quarters around making a small circle. You start to teach this at the halt, when it is understood then you can do it at the walk. Do make sure that you know the word you will be using for this movement. The aim with all that you show and ask your horse to do is that it must be done in a manner that it is as clear as possible for him.

Starting the right turn on the forehand

The easiest way to start this is to stand your horse with his head up to a fence or in a corner. Doing this will help you both because he will not be able to move forward if he misunderstands what you are asking him to do and therefore the only way to go is sideways. You can have a helper at his head to start if you wish, while you work the lunges from the correct position. To begin, you are going to move your horse's quarters off the left aid and toward the right, you are also aiming for him to cross over with his hind legs as he goes.

Standing in the starting position give him a verbal warning 'listen'. Keep an equal feel on the outside rein which on this occasion is the right one, this stops the horse bending too much and walking forwards. Feel on the inside rein so you get a little flexion to the left then tap him with the left rein on the quarter, at the same time giving your verbal aid 'turny'. Even if he only moves one or two steps away from the pressure give him plenty of praise, make sure that you also step sideways as he moves his quarters around. When you have finished walk forward and away, then bring him back to the same position to try again.

Possible problem and correction

If he gets confused then the helper should just tap him on the tummy in the region of the rein, while you are repeating the aids. If you are on your own, ask him to 'stand', keep talking to him while walking up his nearside taking up the lunges as you go. Place the lunges in your left hand then put your hand on the bit and just flex his neck towards you. Facing his shoulder, tap him with your right hand on the tummy or tap the quarters with a whip, at the same time giving the verbal aids. Again, any response must be rewarded but beware of only letting him keep on doing a couple of steps as this could become a habit and when you ask for more, he will not agree. Practise two or three times moving off the left rein and the right one. That would be enough for the session.

You are aiming to build up to a half turn and when that is confirmed move in off the track and you can do a full one. Do think about the balance with the reins, and be careful not to get too much bend in the neck when asking for the flexion. If that happens your horse will not be able to do the movement correctly and will fall out through the shoulder and move sideways.

HALF WALK PIROUETTE

Both you and your horse walk into this movement, then you will stay in the same spot and your horse will perform a small half circle around you going sideways. He needs to leave the track with the shoulders leading a little and when he finishes the movement he arrives at the track with his body parallel to the track facing the other direction.

When doing this movement on the long reins

it is larger than when it is being ridden, so if you have ridden it then try to forget that feeling you have had.

How to start the half pirouette

The easiest starting position I think is to be a couple of strides out of a corner, preferably with a fence or something solid on the outside: by doing this you have taken away one escape route. In other words he can now only go forward which you can control or he can go sideways, where you want him to go. Have your horse standing, give him the verbal warning 'listen' to get his attention. Give him the word for this movement such as 'pirouette' and repeat it during the exercise, feel on the inside rein, to ask for the flexion. When your horse gives the flexion keep a steady contact, this is the directional rein to show him the way round. With the outside rein tap him on the quarter to encourage him to move around and away from it. If he goes to move forward when you touch him on the quarter, half halt on the outside rein and tell him 'no, steady'. Quietly repeat all the aids, do not worry if he moves forwards a little and sideways, it is a start.

As with all the work, in the beginning be satisfied with little, give him plenty of praise. When you have finished, ask him to walk on and then bring him back to repeat the exercise. I often practise things in the same place to start with. I am not too worried if my horse anticipates a little bit because that can often help to get him on the aid, which is making it easier for him to learn.

While you are giving the aids think of keeping this as a forwards and sideways movement and at all costs beware of pulling backwards on the reins. In all the work you do, think of forward movement and allow to happen what you are asking for. Sometimes you need to think of a juggling act with the reins.

Possible problem and correction

It is possible that your horse might get a little confused both with this movement and with the turn on the forehand. The aids to start are the same in that you feel on the left rein to ask for the flexion. This is where it can be a problem if your horse anticipates and is quick to learn but you will also then realise how the voice can help and the importance of having different words for the movements.

Having your horse next to a solid guide line of any description will help him to start the movement because he cannot move out off the track. If he turns his quarters to start the turn on the forehand instead of what you are asking for say a positive 'no'. Keep a positive feel on the inside rein, if necessary drop the rein a little lower and this should stop the quarters turning the wrong way. If you have a helper ask them to stand by the outside shoulder. Ask your horse to 'listen' then your helper, facing the horse, should place their right hand on the bit, the left hand then taps the horse on the shoulder to help move him away. You must keep giving all the aids. Be careful that the inside rein does not restrict the horse coming round to the left. You need to think of almost playing with the reins, asking and allowing with them. This should stop you blocking him if this is a problem.

On your own, there are two ways you can work through this. If you are in the long-reining position get your horse's attention with 'listen' then 'stand', take up the reins and move up to the offside still talking to him. Lead him forwards and round so that his quarters are in a corner, this should help control them. Put the reins into your right hand then place your right hand on

the bit, by doing this the contact stays even. Place your left hand on his shoulder, standing nearer his head so he does not misunderstand and think you want him to do turn on the forehand. Whilst giving him a very clear voice aid push his head gently away from you and tap him on his shoulder, all at the same time.

The other way is to have him on the long reins in the starting position on the left rein; carry a long whip so that you can touch him either on the shoulder or the stifle area, whichever gives the best response. Give him your voice aid 'listen' to get his attention. Combine using your voice directional aid 'pirouette' with feeling on the inside rein to get the flexion. Holding the whip in your right hand keep a steady contact on the rein and tap him on the outside shoulder. Take your time, reward any response.

Often in the beginning stages of learning lateral work people do get into trouble with the coordination of the reins and aids. Remember that, as with everything, some people and horses learn things quicker than others but patience will win.

SHOULDER-IN

This exercise is generally acknowledged as one of the first lateral movements a horse is taught. It helps him to balance, by encouraging him to engage the hind legs under, and it stretches him laterally around his body. It is an exercise that can help to straighten a horse which is going crooked and is used through to the highest levels when training horses for collection.

This is a good comparison for you to see. The height difference shows how the reiner has to use the reins in a different manner, hence the voice work really comes in to effect with the little ones. Jack (above) is showing too much angle through his whole body and he is showing four distinct lines.
(Opposite) Goliath's shoulder-in is more technically correct as he is on three lines. Outside hind is one line, inside hind and outside fore on the same line and inside fore on one line, he could have a touch more bend.

In this movement the horse moves down the track with his head, neck and shoulders on the inside track with the flexion away from the direction he is going while his quarters stay on the outside track. For instance walking on the left rein on the track the horse is asked for a left flexion with the inside rein, the outside rein controls the bend. Imagine now that the horse is going to start a circle, the head, neck and shoulders follow the direction of the bend to start the circle. They leave the track but instead of the quarters following he then carries on going down the track. I say that you should think of the hind feet still pointing down the track as if he was going straight, even though the shoulders are in.

If you were standing in the corner looking up the track you would see the outside hind leg on one line, then the inside hind leg would be on the same line as the outside foreleg, the inside foreleg is on its own line, the horse would be going down the track with a slight bend away from the direction he is moving in. This would be a classically correct shoulder-in moving on three lines. Depending on the horse and handler's ability you will often see in the beginning that the horse moves on four lines, this will usually mean that the horse has too much angle and is straight throughout.

How to start shoulder-in
I do this movement in either of two ways working on short or long reins. You can do this with the outside rein over your horse's back but depending on your ability you may find it is not so easy to keep the flexion that you need for this movement and it is possible that you will lose your horse's quarters and you will get too much angle.

Keeping the reins each side of the quarters

walk through the corner, think of preparing to go onto a circle. Get your horse's attention with a verbal warning 'listen' followed by your voice aid 'shoulder' for the movement. While you do this, feel on the inside rein to ask him to bend a little, the outside rein allows him to move off the track with the front end. It is then used to control the bend and stops your horse walking off to follow the direction he is being given by the inside rein. As your horse comes into the position you want with his shoulders, give a half halt both verbally by saying 'steady' and with a feel on the reins. Gently tap on the inside quarter and this will encourage him to move on down the track in the shoulder-in position. If you feel him losing impulsion then tell him 'forwards' in a brisk manner. All the time give your verbal aids and be ready to ask and allow with the reins during the movement. Aim for a few strides only to start with and as he responds give him plenty of praise.

When you are ready to finish and before he stops offering give him a verbal aid such as 'all right, good boy' the words can be what you want as long as they tie in with that movement finishing. Do not try to bring his shoulders back on to the track as he is not yet ready to do that. Instead allow him to go into a circle or change the rein on a diagonal directly on the line he is aiming for. You should be facing and walking down the track in between your horse's hind footprints. You might find it a little difficult to keep the balance and control to begin with in this movement but as you both find the happy medium it will come.

Possible problem and correction
A common problem that we should cover is too much neck bend, which in turn will cause your horse to fall out through the shoulder while

going down the track. When this happens the reiner will normally also have problems getting the horse off the track. The feel you will have on the reins basically is that the more you try to get him off the track with your inside rein the more his neck comes round, another name for this is 'rubber necking'. While this is happening his body keeps going down the track. This is also a common riding problem.

The priority is to get that shoulder back under control and get your horse equally into the reins. Give him the verbal aid to 'listen and halt', at the same time feel down the reins and as he halts ease the pressure. This is actually quite a common training mistake when the reiners are starting. Too much inside rein when asking the shoulder to come in and the outside rein has been given away. To rectify this go back to square one, do some regular-size turns, circles, changes of rein. Think about your reins and keep equal contact. Then start to make smaller and tighter turns, if your horse tries to do what had happened before say a positive 'no, stop it'. Use the outside rein to straighten the neck and tap him with the inside one – that should do the trick.

When trying the shoulder-in again have your horse going well into both hands and, maybe carrying a whip, walk a small circle but keep him straight in it, as you come back to the track do not even think about flexion. The aim is to do a very shallow shoulder-in (we would call it shoulder-fore), think of the circle and ask him with the inside rein. Give him the verbal aid 'listen, shoulder'. Be very aware of the outside rein, do not give it away in an effort to bring the horse off the track. Allow with your fingers so that he follows the direction. Because you are making a correction it is important that you are aware of keeping him straighter through his neck so that he cannot bend too much again whilst he is doing this movement. As he follows the direction you have asked him to go in, think of the feel you have on the reins and use the outside one to control the bend and the inside one to tap him over. Be content with a few strides done correctly with you being able to control the neck and the shoulder.

TRAVERS

In this exercise the horse walks down the track and, while keeping the correct bend and looking in the direction he is going, he is asked to bring his quarters in off the track. The head, neck and shoulders all stay on the track, there is not any crossing over of the front legs only the hind ones. He goes on two tracks or three lines. The most important part of this exercise is that the horse is looking in the direction that he is going. Once my horse has mastered travers and renvers then I will move onto half pass on the diagonal. When starting this work it is often the reiner not the horse who has a problem going forwards and sideways whilst keeping the correct bend. Mastering these two movements will help you to get the coordination together, therefore making everything much easier for all concerned.

Starting travers

The easiest way for your horse to understand your request for this movement is to start it either when finishing a circle and just as you hit the track or when coming out of a corner. By doing it either of these ways your horse is already being set up with the bend that is needed for this movement.

As your horse goes through the corner, warn him that you are about to do something. Say

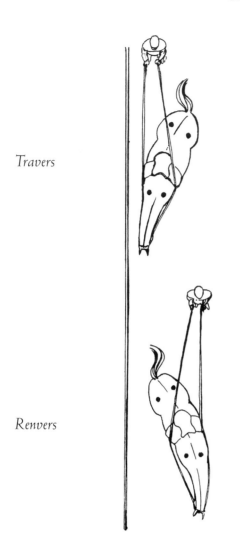

Travers

Renvers

You can see very clearly here the positioning required and the difference between both movements.

'steady, listen' then quietly lift the inside rein up and over his back. You need to be ready to ask for the quarters to come in before he is on the straight coming out of the corner. With both hands now on the offside of your horse, keep an equal contact on the reins. Feel with your fingers on the inside rein, this will ask him to give to the inside and makes sure you do not get a wrong bend. While you are doing this drop the outside rein a little lower and touch him on the barrel or stifle area. At the same time as you give the rein aids give him the verbal one 'travers' and no matter how little the response give him plenty of praise. You may find that he only offers to move his quarters in a little bit then straighten up. That is fine, it is a start. Before you attempt any more steps, take him into a small circle which again will help set him for the movement, much the same as coming through a corner.

To bring him out of the travers give him the verbal aid 'all right, straight', and, with the reins, bring the outside one back up so that it is level with the inside one. By doing this it has released the quarters to go back on the track. To make it very clear, and until your horse totally understands that he can straighten up, slide the inside rein over towards his inside hip and just give it a light touch. While you are doing this repeat your verbal aids. When he responds I would then ask him to halt and make much of him. For all the work you will do with your horse it is always a fine balancing act with the reins – ask and allow, be aware of stopping your horse completing what he is being asked to do.

Possible problem and correction
Being able to keep the horse flexed in the direction he is going seems to be a fairly common problem. What happens is that the reiner has too strong a hold on the outside rein, consequently it is impossible for the horse to look where he is going and he ends up with his nose facing the wall or else totally bent the wrong way. This can also happen if the horse is stiff and finds bending difficult. Doing the following exercise if your horse is stiff will help

him, if he is not it will give you an idea of how to feel on the rein when asking your horse to go into travers.

Standing by your horse's shoulder, put your nearest arm over his withers, hold a lunge in each hand as if you are riding him and feel on one rein then the other. Do not 'saw' his mouth, spend some time on each side, opening and closing your fingers so that you are talking down the reins to his mouth. You need to 'wake up' his mouth in case your hand has been too heavy and he has stopped listening to the rein. Talk to him as well, when he responds and starts to answer you by relaxing his jaw praise him but then ask him to bend a little as well for a moment then straighten him up and repeat the other way.

Be careful that you do not ask too much to start with, otherwise he will tip his nose in an effort to do what you are asking. As he loosens up it will be easier to do.

Next time you practise the travers be positive that you give a good feel on the inside rein as you are coming through the corner, get a nice flexion and allow your horse to look in the direction he is going. Remember to feel and allow, work the inside rein, drop the outside one and tap him on the stifle while all the time using the voice. As he responds, try not to keep asking with the rein aids, let him do it.

RENVERS

The easiest way to explain renvers is to ask you to picture your horse standing in travers position with the wall on the nose side. Keeping the horse in the same place move the wall over to his other side, so now his bottom is on the outside track and his shoulders are on the inside one.

Your horse is still in the same position but it is reversed, in as much as he is bent and looking in the direction he is moving in. The front legs do not cross over but the back ones do.

To bring your horse into renvers I would suggest that you use the walk pirouette as a preparation to start as this does have your horse flexed in the direction that he is moving in. As you are finishing a left pirouette, bring the left rein up over his back and about two strides before your horse reaches the track, give a half halt on the right rein and tell him 'listen, steady' at the same time feel on the left rein so you keep the flexion. Drop the right rein down your horse's quarters a little and lightly tap him with it. The quarters should now be moving over to the track and because you are giving half halts on the rein the shoulders are on the inside track. Praise him while he is doing this and encourage him to move on down the track. Give the verbal command 'renvers' and do not stop your horse moving forward during this manoeuvre. It is not as complicated as it sounds. To bring him out of it bring the right rein back to its normal position and say 'all right, forwards'. Ease the left rein over to his left hip and touch him with it and feel on the left rein, allow with the right one and he should follow his nose back to the track. Alternatively, ease off the outside rein, feel the inside rein and say 'all right, straight' – so that as he moves onto the diagonal line you are following. When done, bring him to halt and make a fuss of him with plenty of praise.

Possible problem
The main problem you might find with this is the same as in the travers so read that section.

REIN-BACK

By all accounts your horse should be well on the voice aid for this movement so warn him that you are going to ask him to do an exercise by telling him 'listen and halt'. If you need to use the reins feel on both at the same time, this way your horse will stay straight as he halts. Praise him when he responds, ask him to wait, do not be tempted to go into rein-back the minute he halts as he could start to anticipate this movement and fidget. For the rein-back I say 'listen and back'. To start I give a feel down the reins and as soon as my horse answers by stepping back I only use the voice. When he has done enough steps I will say 'all right, halt', taking the reins up as I go to one side of him. I keep talking and pat him. Again this stops him anticipating the move off. When I am ready I will walk back, wait a minute then say 'listen, walk on'.

Possible problem and correction

This could be that your horse goes back crooked and might be caused because you are giving too strong an aid with one rein, or his hips are too close to the side. In an effort not to hurt himself he will bring his quarters in off the track, very sensible really! Be aware of where you are asking him to do this exercise. If that is not the case, then you are possibly asking too strongly with one rein so causing your horse to rein-back away from the rein. When asking him to come back think about the feel you are getting from your horse's mouth – is it equal? If not ask him to walk forward into the reins then ask him to halt and flex him to the left then the right. Now ask him to come back again. If he goes to step sideways into the lunge be ready to tap him with it and say 'no'. As he responds praise him. Repeat the exercise again but be ready to correct him the minute he goes off line, then leave it. Finish with a lot of praise.

WHAT NEXT?

I have put down all these exercises which will help you to educate your horse's mind, make his body supple and enable him to carry himself in a more balanced way of going. It is now up to you what you do with them. You can make up programmes where the movements are related to each other. Try bringing in different things to do with your horse: you could make your own obstacle course. We go over banks, through water, over plastic and you could even try backing your horse through parallel poles as done in the Western work. I really do feel that this work benefits horses of all ages especially if you are re-schooling a horse maybe from race work. Remember your goals through this work are that your horse should be accepting the bit and working in a way that will benifit him. The important part is that you both enjoy it and learn an interesting New Sensation. At the end of your work always let your horse stretch and relax before you put him away.

PART 4

GET STARTED WITH DRIVING

INTRODUCTION

I have added the driving section because of the amount of interest shown at our training days and Roadshows. Often when a pony is outgrown he is either left in the field, given away on loan or sold.

This section is not written with a view to you buying the 'ideal' type of driving horse or pony but to show you how the one you already have can hopefully do the job, thereby giving it a new lease on and objective in life.

I also feel that driving is a good outlet for people of any age who may not want to or cannot ride for whatever reason, it is also possible for carriages to be adapted in order to take wheelchairs. One lady driver with whom I spoke told me that driving gave her a freedom that following her accident she thought was gone forever. Because of her injuries it was not possible to ride again even in a special saddle. I have only admiration for anyone who overcomes illness or disability which has changed their life irrevocably and who looks for another outlet in which to channel their energies.

When debating whether or not your horse could take to driving it is necessary to take certain aspects into consideration. Nine times out of ten driving involves going out onto the road and I would consider it highly dangerous to take a traffic-shy horse out, he really should be as bombproof as possible. In temperament he should be willing and cooperative, it could well be impossible to try to work a horse who is tense, worried and nervous. This might also be a reason why you don't really like riding him and if that is the case let him go on to a happier situation with a new rider.

The size of your equine friend determines what weight he can pull, if he is a mini then he will realistically only be able to take one person, unless of course you have two of them.

Don't forget that donkeys and mules can also be used, many of which I have seen just standing in the fields.

After one of our demonstrations I heard from a lady who said that she was so inspired by the different 'Sensations' that she decided to have a go with her eighteen-year-old cob. He was fit as well as active and had great attitude, so after much preparation work at home she then took him to a professional trainer to actually put him to and for the initial drives. He has taken to it like a duck to water and she has been competing with him.

Hercules and me taking a trip down the lane.

LESSON 16

WHAT IS NEEDED TO GET STARTED?

THE VOICE

I have put this first because I think this is the most important item that you will need if you wish to drive your horse. That may seem a strange statement when you obviously have the reins but your horse cannot see you when he is wearing blinkers but he can hear you. I have spoken to many leading Whips (drivers) on this issue and they have endorsed it one hundred per cent.

THE HARNESS

If you have made the decision to have a go with driving then I would strongly recommend that you take a few runs just to check that you do enjoy it before you invest in a set of harness. Whilst you can do the lungeing and long reining with the equipment you have, you will really have to use a set of harness for the next stage. There are some very reasonably priced ones available in either a very strong webbing or leather, and do not forget the second-hand market but do make sure it is well checked over from whichever source it comes from. Sometimes you even find that friends have some harness tucked away.

SAFETY ASPECT

It is sensible for any handler to wear hat and gloves. I also make a habit of carrying string in case of breakage and a knife as well to cut things free. Yet those extra items would not have helped my friend who was competing at a major trial with a team of four. When going through a hazard the leader bar broke. She was holding the reins in both hands and the next thing she realised was that she was being pulled clear over the wheelers landing face down in front of them. The leaders took off as they were free, while the wheelers and the cart went straight over my muddied friend. It does seem a rather hazardous sport, fortunately both four-legged and two-legged beings survived.

Wherever you start your horse make sure that access all around is clear, so if anything happens you lessen the risks to the horse and yourself.

WEIGHTS TO PULL

Initially your horse will start with a person placing some weight on the traces. As he takes and copes with this he will then move on and have a lightweight plank or the like placed behind him. I also use other types of materials such as a tyre and anything that makes a noise as it moves over different ground from gravel to concrete. Make sure that you have long enough ropes or lunges which you will use to connect the tyre to the traces with enough to spare as it comes back to the helper's hand, who will release it if there is a problem. If you have a harrow this can be useful to get him used to pulling a heavier object. The more preparation you do before he is put to a cart can only help build this trust and confidence in what he is being asked to do.

If you use long traces to pull the weight, do not make the mistake a friend of mine made. The reins were not quite long enough so they decided to stand between the horse and the log which was fine until the horse took fright and went. The reins were eased out but they forgot to jump out of the way of the log which hit them behind the legs and sent them flying. A lesson to be learnt.

WHIPS

It is strongly recommended that all drivers carry whips. Sometimes you may just need to touch your horse if he is slow to react to your verbal aid, or if you are having a problem then the whip takes the action of your leg. Finally you will need to use it for your signals if you are going on the road.

There are different types of whip available and it is important that you handle it well before buying one. It must feel comfortable in your hand and not be too heavy as it could make your wrist ache. It should be well balanced, otherwise you will find that it is a struggle to keep it in the right position in your hand. The length of the whip depends on your horse's size. A rough guide is that the stock, the solid part, should be about three feet six inches (1.1m) for a small pony going up to four feet (1.2m) for a cob. For a larger horse the stock would go to five feet (1.5m) and in all cases the thong is about four feet (1.2m).

LEG PROTECTION

I do not use anything on their legs once the horses are going but I do think that it is sensible in the initial stages when your horse is getting used to the harness, just in case he gives himself a bang.

LESSON 17

PARTS OF THE HARNESS AND TRAP

THE BRIDLE

You might be tempted to use an ordinary bridle which is called an 'open' bridle but it is best to get a purpose-made one. The main difference is that a purpose-made one, known as a 'closed bridle', will have blinkers. They stop the horse seeing the wheels behind him or any other objects which could frighten him and they will also help to keep his concentration on you and keep him listening to your voice and rein aids. In the event of an accidentally mishandled whip they will protect his eyes. Blinkers come in different shapes and they can be round, square, dee- or hatchet-shaped. Basically it is down to personal preference and seeing which one suits your horse but they should be sufficiently convex in shape and it is important they fit correctly. The blinkers are stitched onto the bridle and the winkerstay is an adjusting strap which buckles in the centre of the head piece. This is used to move the blinkers in or out depending on the horse. It is important that they fit well against the horse's face but they must not press onto the eyes or hinder his forward vision.

The noseband is not always a separate strap as with an English bridle but usually the cheek pieces will fit through hoops on the noseband or the noseband fits through hooks on the cheek piece. Due to the size of my miniatures' heads I tend not to use nosebands at all, in fact they were not supplied with my bridles when I bought them.

A sensible precaution, particularly if you are going out on cross-country work, would be to put a headcollar under the bridle and we always carry spares and a knife in case of an emergency.

THE BIT

There are many bits available producing different types of action and depending on what sort of driving you wish to do, from showing to cross-country. The most widely used appears to be the Liverpool driving bit which can have a variety of mouth pieces – smooth, thin, jointed and unjointed. It can have either fixed or swivel cheeks – it really is a very versatile bit. In the plain cheek position there is no curb action but

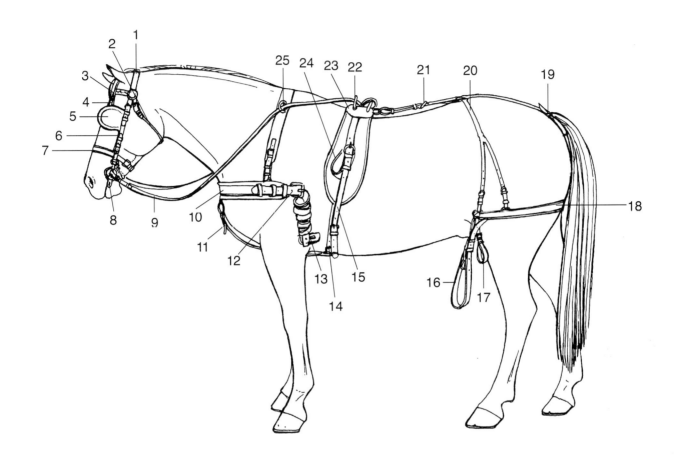

Parts of the Harness

1	Headpiece	8	Liverpool bit	15	Bellyband	22	The terrets
2	Throat lash	9	Reins	16	Breeching straps	23	The driving pad or
3	Browband	10	Breast or Dutch collar	17	Trace bearer		saddle
4	Winkerstay	11	False martingale	18	Breeching	24	The shaft tugs
5	Blinker	12	The hame tug	19	The cropper	25	Rein terret
6	Cheekpiece	13	The trace	20	The loin strap		
7	Noseband	14	Girth strap	21	The back strap		

Hercules posing in a closed (blinkered bridle) but with no breeching on the harness.

as you move down the different rein positions so the action becomes stronger, I tend to place a rubber guard on the curb chain as a matter of course.

For my miniature horses I use an Australian half cheek jointed snaffle, I also use this same bit for long reining and any other work.

THE REINS

I think the reins are very much a personal preference depending on the size of your hands. I like solid fairly wide reins as narrow ones can be a bit difficult to hold in the wet weather. There are many types such as plaited, flat, laced, some even have hand grips sewn on.

The length of rein will depend on the size of your horse and the carriage you are going to drive. Too short and they can be pulled out of

your hands if the horse trips, too long and they tend to get caught up with your feet.

When harnessed, the reins are put through the terrets and buckled onto the bit, the spare reins can be folded up and slotted through the offside terret. If the horse is waiting in the stable, do not connect the reins to the bit. Put the reins through the terret, allow enough to buckle up when ready and attach them safely back on the harness. The spare rein is wrapped and put under the back strap or through the offside terret.

COLLARS

There are two types of collar, the full or neck collar which is the sort that you often see on the big dray horses and the one I tend to use most frequently as it is lighter, particularly for my minis, the breast or Dutch collar. If you are getting this type make sure that it is not narrow and that it is well padded on the inside. When using a breast collar the vehicle must be fitted with a swingle tree onto which the traces will be hooked as this prevents the horse's shoulders being rubbed when he is moving.

THE TRACES

The full collar has hame tugs fixed onto it, these carry a buckle to which the trace is attached or if the trace is sewn on then it will have chain ends or short leather couplings which allow the length to be altered. The traces have a slot called a 'crew' or a 'dart' hole at the other end which slips over the trace hook on the swingle tree or is attached to the vehicle itself.

Breast collars will normally have buckles on each end for the traces to attach to. The traces go underneath the bellyband and through the trace bearers then connect onto the swingle tree.

DRIVING PAD OR SADDLE

The saddle should be well flocked and fits in the same manner as a regular saddle, that is to say there must be good clearance between the spine and the gullet so that you can see daylight at all times, even when girthed up. Serious damage can be caused to a horse's back if fitted incorrectly when the weight of the trap and the driver goes on if the vehicle is not properly balanced.

THE TUGS

For driving a single horse to a two-wheeler it is best to use a sliding backband which passes through a channel in the saddle. The shaft tugs, which are buckled to the backband, support the shafts. The shaft tugs which tend to be used with nearly all two-wheelers are usually the open type, which is a fixed loop. This way when the vehicle is balanced, the shafts ride freely in the tugs.

The French or Tilbury tugs which are fastened tightly around the shaft are normally used with four-wheelers and only occasionally with two-wheelers.

Boysie in an open bridle and harness with breeching.

THE BELLYBAND

This band goes under the stomach and slips through a loop on the girth strap which keeps it in place. There are buckles on each end of the band which go onto the backband which then forms a continuous loop. It should be done up loose enough to allow the tugs some play and it must not interfere with the action of the tugs.

THE TERRETS

On either side of the saddle are the terrets, through which the reins pass. Sometimes they are just metal rings sewn on but the safest are actually screwed into the tree – it all depends on the quality of the harness.

THE CRUPPER

This piece goes under the horse's tail and is either sewn or buckled to the backstrap and is connected to the saddle by a dee ring. The reason for using a crupper is to prevent the saddle sliding forward onto the horse's withers. It is vitally important that the crupper is kept clean, soft and supple or it can make the horse very sore and then cause other problems with the horse anticipating pain when wearing it.

There are two types of crupper: one with buckles called an opening dock, which I think is the better type to work with as it is very easy to fit simply by undoing the buckle and taking it under the tail and then doing it up again, and the closed dock which you have to feed the tail through.

THE BREECHING

This is a long, broad strap which goes around the quarters. The seat of the breeching lies horizontally in line with the stifle joint. It is supported by the loin strap which goes over the horse's quarters and passes through a loop on the backstrap. It is attached to the breeching dees on the shafts by breeching straps. Not all harness has breeching – we have noted this particularly with the miniature horse harness. However, it does prevent the vehicle from running into the horse's quarters particularly when going downhill. Alternatively you can add a 'false' breeching which is a broad leather strap fitted across the shafts about eight to ten inches (20 to 25 cm) in front of the dashboard – this will do the same job of holding the vehicle back off the horse.

BASIC VEHICLE

We will start at the front of the cart and work backwards. The shaft goes through the tug and stops when it reaches the tug stop which is on the shaft. Further along is the breeching dee, the breeching strap will go through this and be buckled back on itself. If using a breast collar, the cart must have a swingle tree fitted. The traces will then be attached to this, the next main piece is the dashboard which may have a mounting handle. This joins the footboard, on the side will be the footstep or mounting step. You then move up to the seat and the back of the seat is called the lazy back.

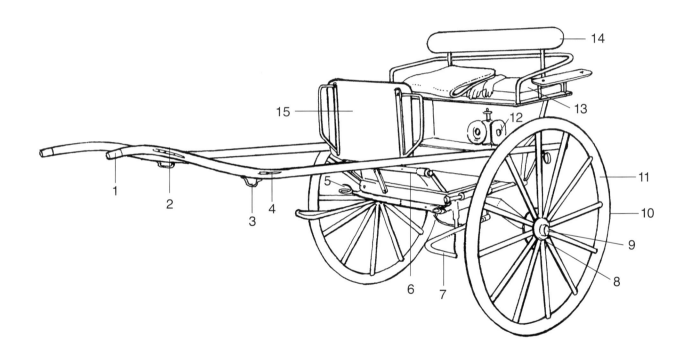

Parts of the Vehicle

1 Shaft tip	5 Swingle tree	9 Hub cap	13 Seat cushion
2 Tug stop	6 Footboard	10 Tyre	14 Seat back
3 Breeching dee	7 Step	11 Felloe	15 Dashboard
4 False breeching dee	8 Hub	12 Lamp	

LESSON 18

PREPARING YOUR HORSE FOR HARNESS

YOUR HORSE

Before you go off and put all the harness onto your horse in one go it is very important to remember that this would be the easiest way to put him off driving for life, and give you a rather difficult time handling your horse. You really need to break down the training programme into stages and it is imperative that you lay down the ground work before even thinking of the vehicle.

As in all the work you do with any horse, treat each one as an individual and take him at his own pace. It does not matter if it takes time, if you try to rush him you could find that he will get worried, lose confidence and possibly panic. In that case you must go back to square one, it is quite simply the only way.

Each section of your programme needs to be thoroughly mastered and understood by both your horse and yourself before moving on to the next stage. Not only is the preparation at the beginning of all your work laying down the roots of all training but it is imperative never to get complacent and start taking your horse for granted. At the same time do not become a nervous wreck anticipating a problem before it happens because then your horse will get feed back from you and will become worried, so it becomes a never ending circle!

Horses have the ability and a sense which allows them to size up or assess each person who handles them. So be warned if you are a worried or nervous driver your horse will pick this up, he will turn the tables around and start to take charge, which could be a dangerous situation.

The interesting side of working with any animals is that they are not machines, they are not predictable. Everything he learns with you will stay with him. Like an elephant, he will remember both the good times and the bad ones. Horses have brilliant memories and I firmly believe have a capacity for flashbacks. Everything you have just read is relevant to all the work and training you will do with your horse. I feel it is especially important because you are wishing to place a vehicle behind him — he needs to understand what is wanted, be listening to you and have the confidence in you to do what you are asking of him, such as approaching and going past objects which might frighten him.

LUNGEING AND LONG REINING

We have discussed the bridle earlier and for all our preliminary work with the harness I use an open bridle. Only when I am happy with the way he is going, accepting the harness and pulling things will I then introduce him to the closed bridle.

I tend to have my horses working well on the lunge and on the long reins before I put the harness on. This way they are well used to having things like lunges hanging and moving around their legs.

The sequence of events is that your horse must be well briefed on the exercises in the lungeing section, happy with the whip work and with the voice aids. It is in your best interests if both of you are also competent on the long reins. From there you will go back to the lunge work and add the crupper first, then the rest of the harness in sections as I will describe. Even though I tie my horses up when they are being either tacked or harnessed up, I do make sure that they will stand free when asked. It can be a pain if your horse will only stand when you are holding him. Practise standing him outside his stable with a headcollar and a lunge on or a bridle and lunge. I use a lunge because if I want to walk around I can feed the lunge out but be in control if he decides to go walk about. Be by your horse's head and stand him up square. Looking at him, hold your hand up, back away from him and at the same time tell him to 'stand', praise him and keep talking to him as you are moving away. If he goes to move put your hands towards him again and strengthen the 'stand'. If needed, give a good feel on the lunge. Over a period of time build up the space between you and also walk all around him, during the whole time keep talking to him. When you get back round to the front make a big fuss of him with plenty of praise.

YOUR CLOTHES

The choice is yours but it is best when doing all work with your horse to wear gloves and a hat and when driving make sure you are wearing good non-slip shoes. It is sensible also for any helpers to wear the correct gear.

FITTING THE CRUPPER

The one thing that might upset your horse is the crupper. To try to make the transition as smooth as possible I sometimes use the following method. Firstly, I tie up my horse and put the saddle on. Then I will untie him and an assistant will come in and hold my horse with a lunge threaded through the tie-up ring and then connected to the headcollar. This way he will not panic if he pulls back or risk hurting himself. All the time I am working with him I am talking to him and stroking him so that he feels relaxed. I connect a long tail bandage to the saddle, take it along his back and standing on the nearside, lift his tail high enough so that I can bring the bandage under the tail taking it back to the saddle and tying if off. I will bring him to the door, let him see me put some food on the floor and then let him loose. This gives him something else to think about and he enjoys it. Do this for a couple of days then put the 'real' crupper on.

I feel it is best if your horse has the saddle and crupper on in his stable for a couple of days

before you take him out to lunge him. Prepare him for tacking up as I have already explained, making sure that all the time you are talking to him, patting him and relaxing him. Depending on the type of crupper you have, fit it as described. For the open dock, the backstrap can be attached to the saddle, then unbuckle one side, lift the tail and bring it under making sure there is no hair caught and do it up again.

The closed one does not undo so make sure you have enough length in the backstrap to allow the crupper to be halfway down the dock for ease of getting on to start with. You will need to twist the tail, fold it back up to the dock and holding it with your right hand feed it through the crupper being meticulous to ensure that no hairs are left caught. Bring the crupper up to the top of the tail and tighten the backstrap so it lies comfortably.

Once your horse is used to the full harness you can place the saddle mid-way on his back when getting ready so that when the crupper is in place you just move the rest forward and fit correctly.

LUNGEING WITH THE CRUPPER

So that you are in control of your horse, use two reins to lunge him with the saddle, the crupper, the bellyband and the tugs. Connect the bellyband to the backband and this secures the tugs, you can then put the lunges through them. Whichever way you lunge have the inside lunge coming straight to your hand but have the outside through the tug. Do not put on side reins as this could upset your horse by putting pressure on the crupper.

It is possible that he will be upset with the crupper, clamping his tail down, humping his back and even kicking for a short while but this is the worst case scenario. On all accounts he must be kept going forward and he needs to learn that it is wrong, so your voice must give positive indication, not screaming or shouting at him but a strong 'no, stop it'. At the same time you need to keep his attention, do some transitions, use your voice telling him to 'steady' and feel on the reins at the same time. As he settles praise him.

Work him on both reins changing the rein as explained earlier.

ADDING THE BREECHING

Only after your horse has accepted the crupper without tensing up and will work on both reins doing transitions is he ready to have the breeching added. Put the breeching on in the stable, connect the breeching straps by any safe means to the tugs. This will secure the breeching and stop it sliding up over the horse's quarters if he should start bucking. Repeat the same work each day so he accepts everything as normal. Give plenty of praise both verbally and otherwise. If you are around the stables I would leave the harness on for as long as possible, so your horse gets used to the feel and the noise of it when he puts his head down or makes a tight turn and basically he gets desensitised.

As with all the work do not put a time limit on when your horse should be doing this or that by. Expect little and the rewards become greater.

ADDING THE BREAST COLLAR AND TRACES

Finally you can add the breast collar and the traces. Place the traces through the tugs and wrap them up. The breeching straps can now be buckled onto the trace hook slot. Your horse will feel a slightly different type of pressure. Give him time to accustom himself to the feel and sound of the harness when moving, as always give your verbal aids before you do anything different: warn him, ask him then praise him when he responds to the request.

TO CANTER OR NOT

As with many things there are two schools of thought as to whether or not a horse should be cantered with his harness on before he goes into the trap. Realistically if your horse has learnt to canter in his normal lungeing and long-reining tack to your verbal aids then that should be enough. If you and your horse are well versed in working in the harness he should be well used to the sounds it makes.

It is thought that if anything should happen and your horse takes fright and goes into a canter, the movement and noise of the harness should not add to the trauma, as he has already had the sensation of the harness on at canter on the lunge. For those who decide they would like to canter, I have covered the aids in the next section. This is all part of really preparing your horse for whatever work you wish to do with him. I hope that as you look back over the work already covered you will find that your horse accepts what you are showing him without worry because of the trust and confidence you

have built up between you during your time together.

UP TO CANTER

When I am riding my horses I always talk to them and use the words for the movement or paces that I am asking them to do. So if your horse is well on the voice aid, canter on the lunge is no problem, if not then read on. It is important that your horse is working in a balanced active trot, this will make it easier for him to make the transition to canter. Make sure that he is working well into the reins taking an easy contact and not pulling. The aids will be his name followed by 'listen' to get his attention. As you tell him to 'canter left' you will need to give a feel on the inside rein, the outside rein must control the bend. You will get a different feel from the canter pace so be ready to allow him to move forward into it. You must be aware of how your arms and hands are feeling. Keep them soft, think about them, talk down the reins with your fingers, do not just hang on for dear life. If he goes off too fast, remember to use your voice to steady him down and give him a good half halt on the reins, praise him as he responds and make sure that you follow him with your hands.

If you do find that when asking him to go into canter he just lengthens his trot strides quietly say 'no, steady', half halt on the reins and ask him again. This time I would touch him on the hock, depending on your ability it needs to be the outside one as the sequence of canter is: outside hind followed by inside hind and outside foreleg together, lastly the inside foreleg which will be the canter lead that you are wanting i.e. left or right.

FORWARD TO TROT

To bring him into trot, warn him with a half halt on the reins then say 'listen and trot' give him praise when he responds. If he does not respond, repeat the request making sure that you are giving him very clear aids both verbally and with the reins. If necessary give a stronger feel on the inside rein and then ease it, do not hang on. Make sure that you do not let his neck bend in, you need to control the bend with the outside rein. As he goes forward to trot praise him and make sure that it is a good active trot. I would do a couple of transitions on each rein then leave it. Make much of him and then leave it, you do not want him to start anticipating the canter work, so beware.

LESSON 19

PREPARING FOR PUTTING TO

LONG REINING

Long reining is a part of the training for driving of which I feel you cannot do too much. If you think about it, driving is after all only long reining from the vehicle and some people call long reining driving anyway. Your horse should be well accustomed to the lunge whip and not be at all worried by having the whip going over any part of his body. As you are going to carry a whip when driving start using it now when long reining your horse using it as necessary to turn or to ask your horse to go forward. Remember that it is only used on the upper part of the shoulder.

You and your horse should be proficient with the various long-reining exercises explained in Part 3 including the lateral work as this is very relevant to driving. Sometimes you will have to make a very tight turn and in this instance you would ask your horse to side pass around. As you can see it is important that he learns this work before he goes between the shafts. Unless you are very quick and able to anticipate a problem which might happen then leave the reins through the tugs. This will give you much greater control particularly if your horse tries to

turn his quarters out against you. As I have said before, analyse any problem, there is normally a very simple solution. For example, make sure you are holding the reins equally and do not have too much bend in the neck, which will make him difficult to turn as he will fall out through the shoulder. You will have caused the problem!

PUTTING ON THE CLOSED BRIDLE

There are two schools of thought as to whether the horse should go into the closed bridle before starting to pull weights or not. I have worked both ways with open and closed bridles and had no problems but much will depend on the horse and his attitude to what is happening behind him.

If you are happy that your horse is responding to all the work that you are asking him to do then he is ready for the closed bridle. When fitting the bridle it is possible that your horse might be a little surprised at the added extras, particularly for the first time. I tend to hold the

Jack is doing a large walk pirouette, all this work is imperative when working with a harness and trap. Establishing these exerises before you start driving makes life much easier for both horse and handler.

bridle in my left hand, then take my right hand under his chin and put my open hand over the bridge of his nose, during this time I am also talking to him saying 'head down' to enable me to put the bridle on more easily especially with tall horses. I do not grab his nostrils. If he goes to lift his head when he sees the new bridle, the pressure against my hand on the front stops it as well as my saying 'no, head down'. Holding the bridle below the blinkers, place it into the right hand, still keeping it over the bridge, and with my left-hand fingers stretched out and balancing the bit I put my thumb in the corner of the mouth and say 'open'. As he opens his mouth I slowly lift the bridle up and guide the bit in, all the time talking to him and praising him. My left hand then holds the headpiece up and my right hand puts the right ear under the headpiece followed by the left ear. I double check that everything fits correctly and ensure there is no forelock or mane caught up anywhere which will make it uncomfortable, possibly making him

shake his head. For this reason I often cut a small bridlepath. Now your horse's vision has been restricted you need to be careful when leading him out of the stable, he might catch his hips if you turn him sharply. Before moving onto pulling weights give your horse plenty of time to get accustomed to being lunged and long reined in his blinkers.

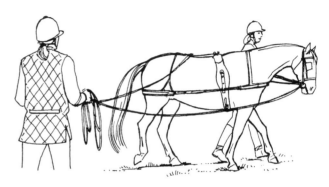

Take your time when your horse first has the closed bridle on as he may be unsure, and have a helper on his outside. Make sure all spare parts of the harness are secure.

Dispense with the assistant at the horse's head only when you are happy with the way the horse is going.

LEARNING TO PULL A WEIGHT

Now that your horse is wearing blinkers and cannot see you the importance of voice training and the voice aids should become very apparent to you. He can only hear your voice and feel the presence of first you, then the other items. The amount of time you spend just settling him, talking to him, working him around and getting him used to wearing the new bridle with the full harness on will all pay dividends. In the beginning I think it is in the horse's best interest to do a steady exercise on two lunges each day before you move on through his training programme.

I think that it is best to have three people on hand for this next piece of training, one will be at your horse's head, you will be long reining and the third person will be assisting with the weights and training objects.

With your horse totally ready in full harness, lead him out to your working area. If possible have someone by his head talking to him and telling him to stand. This is also preparation for when your horse has to stand up when he is in the vehicle waiting to move off. You and your assistant should stroke you horse's neck so he knows you are there and then undo the traces and fix the extra lunge or rope to each trace end, you should extend them by no less than three yards. Have your assistant standing well back holding one in each hand, at this point you do not want them to put weight on the horse's shoulders.

Standing back from your horse in the long-reining position with the reins threaded through the tugs say 'listen and walk on', the traces are just being held up until the horse is walking well and listening to you. Gradually an even pressure can be placed on the traces and the horse is then pulling the person along behind him. Doing it this way the horse gets used to the feel of the collar against his shoulders and going into it, he also feels the traces on his sides and legs.

Keep an even contact with your reins and for

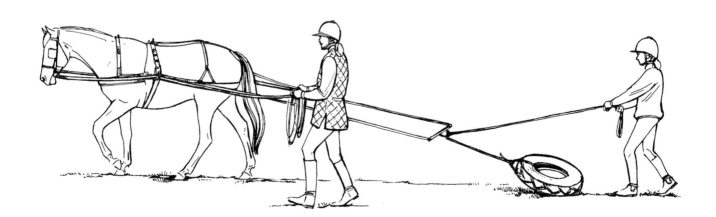

By holding the tyre this way it can be released quickly if needed.

the first lesson work on smooth ground. In walk practise your turns, circles, walk on and halt transitions. Be sure about the words you are using for your aids. Some of my friends use 'away' and 'come by' for left and right. As your lessons with him progress so your assistant needs to pull back against the traces with as much weight as possible. You should now include trot transitions. Keep a steady trot, think about the rhythm as this will be very important when he is in the vehicle. If he keeps altering the speed then, as well as being uncomfortable, he will get tired more quickly.

Let the traces drop around his legs then lift them up, keep talking to him and giving him plenty of praise. It is important that he is not worried by anything moving over, around or under him. Make much of him and do this work until he feels comfortable with it. You also need to let him feel the weight on his shoulders as he moves off from the standstill, as this is how it will be when he is in the vehicle. Remember always to keep your verbal aids the same and as he moves off be aware that you allow him through your hands.

As important as it is that your horse goes forward when asked, it is just as important that he stands and waits when asked. When he is finally in the vehicle and standing with your assistant in front of him, he needs also to learn that he should wait even when the helper has moved away from his front, it can be dangerous if he leaps forward the minute the coast is clear.

There are little things that you need to remember and form as a habit so practise them now. Even on the long reins, I often practise standing my horses up into the contact but not going anywhere. He will know when to move off from that position because I have warned him saying 'listen up, walk on'.

The reason I work in this manner is that if I only take up the contact when I wish to move on then the horse would anticipate the move off as the reins are being taken up and start to move. So whilst it is wrong of him, the problem has started because of me. You need to practise shortening and lengthening the reins but not going anywhere, this applies to all the paces and not only in this discipline – your horse should not alter his way of going unless you ask him to. It all comes down to training.

THE NEXT STAGE

Your horse should now be ready to progress to pulling different objects, this won't really simulate the weight that he will eventually pull but he will get a different feel from them. We use a variety of training equipment such as tyres, logs even a sleeper. Keeping the extra length on the traces you now need to add maybe the tyre to start. In order to stop the traces getting too low on your horse's legs it would be sensible to put a trace bearer over the horse's quarters; when you are doing this have an assistant at his head. Talk to him and stroke him before you start arranging the harness over his quarters, by holding the traces at about stifle height the possibility of your horse putting his leg over the trace when turning will have been taken away. However it is very important that your horse can cope if this does happen and does not panic.

I loop the extended traces together with a rope and whatever I am pulling is also looped through the traces. Nothing is tied together so if there is a problem or the horse gets very frightened I let go of the rope and it just slips apart. If it is light enough, such as the tyre, it can

just be lifted off the ground and when he has settled it is put down again. If you meet a problem talk quietly and calmly to your horse, tell him to 'stand and wait', keep talking to him as you take up the reins going to his head. Make much of him so he does not panic, he knows you will help him as he has confidence in you, your assistant meanwhile can sort out the problem.

A friend who is one of the top Whips in the country told me of how when out schooling one day the carriage hit a stump and flipped over. The young horse was panicking but the older one next to him stood stock still, knowing that help would arrive. An important point that was made was that no matter how experienced you are you should never go out on your own. They were able to sort things out very quickly and in fact due mostly to the older horse's behaviour the young one learnt a very valuable lesson. Horses do copy each other, so if yours is a bit worried in the beginning see if there is an older one around just to walk beside him, he does not have to pull or carry anything.

When pulling the weights practise doing the side turn, again this is in readiness for turning in the shafts. Do this just the same as when long reining but you must be very aware of keeping his neck straight when asking him to 'side', if he bends when in the shafts you will find it difficult to bring him round because you will have lost the shoulder. We have covered in lesson 10 the

problems associated with falling out.

This next piece is a progression from the way your horse has been going, pulling the person behind him. Start him off in exactly the same manner, remembering to give him clear aids and directions with the reins and make sure that whoever is handling the traces and the equipment is alert and competent. Your horse is listening to you so it is important that only you are talking to him when he is moving. As he settles with the equipment behind him doing all the basic exercises you are ready to move off the smooth ground and take him over as many different types of surfaces and conditions as possible. Hopefully you have some hills around you so that your horse gets used to going up and down them, do not go on slippery ones as this will not benefit him at all.

Sounds are important for your horse, the more he is used to noise following him before he is 'put to' (the correct terminology for going into the vehicle) the easier it will be for both of you. You can also long rein your horse and have an assistant following dragging a chain or metal shovel behind but do not connect these to your horse. As with all the work, preparation and patience pays dividends in the end.

Make sure that you do lots of transitions including trotting, turning and just standing still. Talk to your horse, stroke him all the time and this will build up his confidence and trust.

LESSON 20

YOUR PREPARATION FOR DRIVING

MOUNTING THE VEHICLE

The correct way to get into the vehicle is to be on the offside. Have your assistant standing in front of the horse and they must stay there until you are ready to ask your horse to move off. Take the reins with your right hand from where you had placed them. Keep them in your right hand while mounting the vehicle. The nearside rein goes under the index finger and the offside rein under the middle finger, the spare rein is looped and carried on the little finger. When mounting the vehicle hold the handle on the dashboard with your right hand, place your left hand on the body of the vehicle. Put your right foot on the step and step up quickly, quietly and sit down immediately on the offside. During this whole procedure I will say to my horse 'listen, stand up and wait'.

THE WHIP

The whip should be in the whip holder or if your vehicle does not have one then rest the bottom end of it on the footboard leaning up against the seat in the middle. Take it into your hand when you are seated.

However experienced you are, sometimes you do something and then in hindsight say 'never again'. I did promise not to reveal the name of the Whip involved so I won't! The driver had two big young cobs in training ready to drive out. Realising the whip had been left in the stable they dismounted to stand at the horses' heads to hold them while the groom went to get it. The youngsters became fidgety and kept pushing forward, suddenly my friend found that they were being pushed backwards and that the horses were taking control. The last thing they remembered was that the horses pushed on and went straight over them – vehicle and all. They said in hindsight they should have stayed in the carriage, it would have been easier to have kept the horses under control.

YOUR HANDS AND THE REINS

As soon as you are seated transfer the reins across to your left hand which is facing across your body and level, put the nearside rein over your index finger bring the offside one through and under the middle finger, the spare part of the reins hangs down.

The whip is carried in your right hand at an angle of forty-five degrees and facing slightly forward, you use the right hand with the whip to make signals and to assist the left hand when turning as needed. Always keep the reins in the left hand, it is not accepted to drive with one rein in each hand – unless you are doing a particular type of work for competition.

The feel you give down the reins is very important to your horse – always keep a steady, confident contact. Think about how the reins are feeling in your hand, be careful that you do not grip or hold them tightly, otherwise it will cause your arm to be rigid. This in turn will make the horse very wary regarding his mouth and not

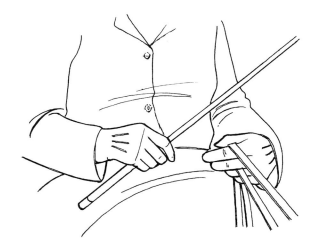

Correct hand and rein position.

sure about going into the bridle or taking the bit. You have to allow him to move through your arm and hand the same as with riding and long reining. Either increase the pressure or ease it off but do not drop it, an inconsistent rein or hard, rigid hand is bad news to any horse and his mouth. Contrarily, a soft, light hand does not constitute a loose rein, with fingers barely holding the reins: it is all about feel and that is something that can be learnt. If you have problems get an expert to help you.

YOUR POSITION

It is important that you have good visibility when you are driving, if the seat is too low then your vision is impaired but it is possible to use a wedge seat or a cushion which will help tremendously. If the seat is too high, then your position might not be as stable as required. Ideally you should be sitting with your back comfortably straight, holding your head up looking where you are going. Keep your arms relaxed and close by your sides with your forearms horizontal. There should be enough leg room in front of you for your legs to be stretched with a slight bend in your knees. Make sure that the footboard is not slippery and you can get a good grip on it, most people prefer a sloping, as opposed to a flat, floor.

THE AIDS

We have covered the basic aids in the long reining, the principles are still the same even though the reins are secured in the left hand and

supported when needed by the right hand. You ask and you allow. It is worth practising holding the reins in this way before you take them up on your horse, either get a friend to hold them or tie them onto something solid. Now you can practise the turning aid, it will be much easier on your horse if you know where you are going before you ask him to do it!

So, holding the reins as already explained with the whip in your right hand you are going to ask to go left. Turn your hand over towards you as if you are looking at your watch; this will tighten the left rein and ease the right, so your horse can follow the directional aid to the left. To turn right, turn your hand again (to look at the watch) now to put more pressure on the right rein just flex your wrist towards you and dip the thumb down a little to the left side. This will then release the pressure on the left rein.

If there is a problem and you need extra help on the rein or you need to alter the rein length then do it in the following manner, still holding the whip in your right hand. Place your right hand in front of the left about six to ten inches (15 to 25cm) up the reins. Take the offside rein through between your third and little finger. Bring the right hand back towards your stomach, allow your horse to follow the direction by giving the nearside rein if you need to, particularly if you are doing a very tight turn. Don't forget your turning words as well.

To lengthen or shorten, place your right hand in the same position and take the nearside rein between index and middle finger, slide your left hand up or down the reins as required. When you are finished take your right hand back to the correct position.

LESSON 21

PUTTING TO AND YOUR FIRST DRIVE

THE VEHICLE

There are specially designed training carts or you can use a two-wheeler which has extra long shafts with a low centre of gravity, as this should help to make the vehicle stable. When not in use the shafts should be placed on a shaft stand as this will keep the vehicle horizontal. If you are going to buy a vehicle make sure that you have an expert with you as there are many different types on the market, your choice depends on what you want to do. There are also reputable companies or Light Harness Horse Instructors (LHHIs) who give advice regarding driving and vehicles. The most important point of all is that the vehicle must fit your horse.

BALANCING THE VEHICLE

You can only really balance the vehicle when the driver and groom are seated. The balance is sometimes altered by moving the seat backwards or forwards, some vehicles have a handle to do this. The floor should be parallel to the ground,

with the shafts lying easily in the tugs. If you lift the shaft tips it should feel very light with no weight on them.

THE FIT OF THE HARNESS AND VEHICLE

The traces are said to be in draft when the horse is pulling the vehicle or if you push back the vehicle they are also in draft. The tugs and backband should not move from their position of lying centrally on the saddle panel when the traces are in draft. When the horse is harnessed up to the vehicle and the traces are in draft there should be a hand's width between the quarters and the seat of the breeching. Gently bring the vehicle forward to check that the breeching comes into action on the quarters before the tugs take any weight and are pushed forward when going down hill.

When harnessing up to drive, do remember to connect all parts correctly and not with string!

The cart's shaft tips should be level with the point of shoulder, the height can be altered by

This is an American training cart for the miniatures.

moving the tug buckles. There should be about two inches (5cm) between the horse and the shafts and roughly eighteen inches (45cm) between the horse's tail end and the closest part of the vehicle.

PUTTING TO FOR THE FIRST TIME

Unless you have done this part before, in which case you most probably will not be reading this book, I would say that you must have someone who is experienced with this sort of work on hand at least for the first few times your horse is being 'put to' or you might even send your horse to a professional to finish. That might seem extreme but I feel that it would not be right or

sensible to try and underplay how serious this next bit can be. You definitely need three people on hand in case there are any hiccups.

Before you 'put to' make sure your horse has a good steady exercise first. Think about the weather and if it is wet and windy, forget it. No, that is not the easy way out but you do want to give your horse every possible chance and both of you will need to have your concentration in order.

Have the vehicle standing ready in the area you are going to work in, there needs to be plenty of space with nothing in the way and it should not be muddy. Prepare your horse: ask him to stand him up square, have one assistant in front of his head. Double check that the girth strap is done up tightly enough. Remember he cannot see behind so keep talking to him and

If you have done your homework with your horse he should accept putting to but do be ready just in case.

stroking him while you unroll the traces and put a piece of strong cord in the trace end so it is ready for use. I do not connect these directly to the swingle tree or trace hook but I tie them with a quick release knot. Place them over the backstrap and undo the breeching straps so they are hanging down. If you have a bellyband which needs to be wrapped several times around the shaft, such as in the American harnesses, I punch an extra hole in it higher up the strap so that I only need to do one wrap in this situation. Safety is the main objective and a quick exit is essential. Have the reins either looped through the nearside terret or placed under the backstrap on the nearside, this is much easier than trying to sort out your horse as well as holding the long reins, I like to make things as simple and as safe as possible. Life does not need to be made difficult for our horses.

Quietly bring the trap up behind him talking to him at the same time. The horse must not back up, the trap is always brought to the horse. Keep talking to him and stroke his quarters as the shafts are being brought forward, this way if one touches his quarters he will not be startled. Go through the tugs until the tug stops are reached,

take the traces through the trace bearers and connect them to the swingle tree or the trace hooks with the quick release knot. The belly-band should be done up tightly enough to prevent the shafts moving, as this could worry a green horse. If you have the wrap system do only one wrap around the shaft. Keep talking and praising your horse. The breeching straps should now be fastened around the shafts, this will stop the trap rolling forward and hitting the horse on the hocks – not the best introduction for the novice horse! Some trainers also use a kicking strap. This goes over the horse's loins and is connected to each shaft. The theory is that the horse should not be able to lift his quarters up to kick.

THE MOVE OFF

Once everything is in place stand back, walk around and double check it all. If you are satisfied then proceed. Standing on the nearside you should now take the reins and stand beside the vehicle, your assistant who was at the head can go to the offside still keeping their rope or lunge on, the third assistant can stand either by the off shaft or behind the vehicle.

To move off say to your horse 'listen', feel on the reins and then tell him to 'walk on', at the same time your assistants must be ready to move the vehicle forward to help your horse. It will be a heavier weight than he is used to and if he finds it difficult to move it from the halt then this can cause a problem called 'jibbing'. It is your responsibility to make it as easy as possible for him to learn this work, remember that. As soon as you are happy with your horse walking round then the outside leader can feed out the lunge a little bit and stay back by your horse's shoulder.

Only you must talk to your horse and keep the words the same as the ones you used on the lunge work. Make all the turns very wide, use your voice. Feel on the inside rein and allow with the outside but do not give all contact away. It is exactly the same as when long reining.

If for any reason he becomes upset or unsettled, calm him with your voice and ask him to halt. Your assistant should go back to his head and you take up your reins while reassuring him with your voice, stroke his quarters and work your way up to his head. Make much of him and, when he is ready, quietly go through the procedure again.

We believe that it is better to work for two short periods of say fifteen to twenty minutes than to overload his brain and muscles. If you can only do fifteen to twenty minutes once a day do not worry. Even if he goes very well the first time do not be tempted to go longer even if you are only doing one session a day. This is a common mistake people often make in all types of work with horses. Do not be greedy! As he progresses with his understanding of what is wanted and he becomes physically fitter so the work programme can get longer.

It is very important that your horse becomes used to the feel of the shafts against his body, so, as soon as we reckon that he is comfortable with everything, I hold the reins and stand back beside the vehicle and have one person by his head and another by the offside shaft. I then ask my horse to 'side' at the same time as the person by the shaft just pushes it against the horse a little at a time. He then becomes used to the feel of the shafts touching and pushing him. It is preparation for what will happen and it is sensible to practise this before you mount into the vehicle when your horse would also have the weight to contend with.

UNHARNESSING FROM THE VEHICLE

You need to be just as careful with this – do not take your horse for granted and assume that because he has been well behaved this will continue. He is not a machine and he could easily get frightened. You are only human and may well do something differently.

Make sure that you bring your horse to a halt on flat ground. If he is a little sharp or worried then it might be sensible to face him into something solid but not too close. When preparing to halt keep your eyes open and decide at what point in your working area you are going to halt. You and your assistants all need to be ready before you tell your horse. Prepare your horse to halt by feeling on the reins, warn him with 'listen and halt'. Your assistant on the outside will move round to the front of the horse's head, then stand in front and hold him. You should take up and loop the reins as you move forward then place them through the terret or under the backstrap. Your second assistant should undo the same parts as you. Talk to your horse all the time. If you have used a kicking strap undo this first, otherwise, starting in the order of bellyband first, unbuckle the breeching straps and lastly the traces; place the traces over the top of the horse or under the backstrap. Do not let your horse walk away when unharnessed from the vehicle, he must always stand still while it is rolled backwards out of the tugs and then placed on its stand. Make sure all the parts of the harness are rolled up and cannot catch your horse on the legs or be trodden on, then make much of your horse and take him back to his stable.

WHAT NEXT?

When your horse has reached the stage that he is working in the vehicle and going through all the basic work that he did on the long reins without any hiccups, then I would feel that he is ready to pull you in the vehicle. The first time I get into the vehicle I do it one of two ways depending on the horse. One way is that I will get into the vehicle from the offside while the horse is walking and all the time I am talking to him. In this way he gets accustomed to the weight slowly. My assistant will have a lunge on the horse just in case something happens and walks beside him to start with. As time progresses with my horse getting stronger and more confident the assistant will then get into the vehicle but still carrying the lunge, this I do for both ways.

The alternative way is for my horse to be standing with an assistant in front of him, I will take up the reins and mount up from the offside, all the time talking to my horse. I also have someone at the back of the vehicle to give it a push as I ask my horse to walk on. This helps to take the weight off his shoulders but I do this only for the first few times.

One comment that has been made regarding newcomers to driving is that, if a problem occurs which necessitates the helper having to get down off the back of the vehicle, it has been noted that they face the back. Because of the momentum, their legs are taken away and they land on their knees. Remember, therefore, always to face the front and keep walking or running as you step off.

This is literally getting you started in driving. You must remember to be patient, there is still much to be learnt, and you will both progress. As with all the work we have done you cannot

Hercules still ready to go.

rush any of it, if there is a problem take time out and analyse it. Above all never forget your voice.

HERCULES KNOWS BEST!

Leading Whip Pippa Thomas agreed to lend a hand at one of my demos in order to give me time to get changed. I said that I would supply all that she needed including the horse.

Even though she now drives a big team, Pip cut her teeth on ponies so I couldn't foresee any problems but I hadn't reckoned with Hercules. Firstly it was cold outside and he thought he had finished work, so he was not in the mood to be very cooperative. Boy, did he let her know! Pip

was facing the audience and explaining how you should only use a well-mannered, sensible horse with the right attitude. Suddenly the audience roared with laughter, she turned around to see Hercules rearing up and putting his front legs around the handler's neck! After he was prised off, he was quickly put to work although he was only on four legs for very short periods of time. This was clearly a case of him deciding to show that he was in charge; when he went into the cart he behaved like a roaring lion. Pip handled it really well and explained that they were seeing how to cope with problems and that with hindsight he should have been lunged for a good while before she worked him. At the next demo he behaved like an angel for her after she had given him a good exercise before her section started.

PART5

GET STARTED WITH
WESTERN RIDING

INTRODUCTION

In the UK Western riding tends to be presented in either competition or pleasure form and it is important to remember that in certain parts of the US the cowboy and his horse are a way of life; working with the cattle is very much in evidence. Fortunately for them there are some things that four wheels just cannot do. Also there are people who are concerned about keeping their history alive and tying it in with the tourist business, which I am very much for. They do this by offering what they call ranch or dude holidays, this is so the regular folk can go and have the experience of working with the cattle and horses.

Alongside the cowboy are the Native Americans – the Indians – and the history of both is kept alive by the rodeos which involve competitions and demonstrations. Many of the breed shows feature Western competition classes, particularly the Appaloosa and the Quarter horse breeds. The movements that are performed in the ring originated from the cowboy and his work on the range.

Western riding is still a relatively small sport in the UK and it is possible that it may never grow to its full potential for the simple reason there are so many other long-standing equestrian disciplines available for riders to do. Before you invest in a Western saddle I suggest that you have some rides in one first, so that you know whether or not you like the actual feel it gives you.

There are professional trainers in the UK who give demonstrations and hold courses for both competitive and leisure riders to promote and expand knowledge of the sport. It might be worth attending some of these but do check that the person is qualified to present this work. You will find at the back of the book some useful addresses to point you in the right direction.

I first rode Western when I lived in the States many years ago and did not really know what to expect. I had the image of the old cowboy films in my mind. Surprise, surprise! Forget any preconceived ideas you might have of horses galloping with their mouths wide open and with their riders swinging on the reins. You might see this when horses are ridden badly but that is no different to seeing anything done incorrectly and it can be enough to put you off. For me as with everything in life (unless it goes against my principles or is crazy dangerous) I will try it once. By doing things this way, I can give a positive reason why when I say 'never again'! It is easy just to say 'no' and life is too short.

I would strongly recommend Western riding

for anyone who wishes to ride purely for pleasure, particularly men. I base this observation on the comments that have been made to me when I have been giving lessons to mixed groups of novice riders. Those who have ridden English first found the structural differences of the saddles quite surprising, possibly due to the width across the seat and the swell of the Western saddle which makes it more comfortable. I have noticed over the years that English saddles seem to be getting narrower. This brings the weight-bearing area into a smaller location which in turn will damage the horse's back. Also, according to many statistics, the lower regions of many people are spreading, so the balance does not seem correct if the load-bearing surface is getting smaller!

To explain the feeling of this type of riding in such a manner that will make you want to have a go just might test and stretch my descriptive abilities but I will try. Imagine that you are sitting in an armchair of a saddle that has a good broad seat which spreads the weight-bearing area over your horse's back and your legs are hanging down at a comfortable angle. Your horse's way of going is very soft, on a loose rein, and he carries himself well, being responsive, supple and listening to you. This is the essence of Western.

Just about everyone who comes on our courses is surprised at the different types of horse used and the work we put them through. It is not difficult work and is basic but they cannot always understand how the work can help any horse. I believe that doing something different with your horse, even if you decide not to follow the whole process through but just take parts of it, can be very beneficial to any horse no matter what work he does. Mentally it will keep him fresh and stimulated and if you do some of the

Idolo and me working over the bank. He would not be considered the 'ideal' type as he is tall and leggy, yet he is a pleasure to ride in Western.

supling exercises plus the trail work this can actually help your horse with muscular development, balance and the flexion of his joints. You will also find related exercises in the long reining part of this book.

One of the comments often made to me concerns the bits that are used, particularly those with the long shanks and this area is covered in more detail in lesson 23. Do not

panic, these bits are not a standard requirement for Western, in fact you can ride Western or English with no bridle at all as long as your horse is well on the aids, particularly the voice!

CAN MY HORSE OR PONY LEARN WESTERN?

The right type

All around the world there is a whole range of riding disciplines, from show jumping and long-distance riding to Western. Each has its own individual style suited to the work it has been developed for and in most cases the horses are selected to do the job required. I would say that while Western riding emerged from the work on the ranches, it also encompasses the rider's position, the tack, the way of going and the work performed.

In certain lines of work, horses are bred specially with attributes that are best suited to the training for and the ability to perform the job required. The Western horse has been bred to suit the work he was and is used for on the range. Amongst the best known are the Quarter horse and the Appaloosa and each has its own characteristics of conformation, size and temperament that make it suitable for Western work. Like a purpose-made car they are built for the job, and amongst other things they have the body and the 'engine' to enable them to work properly over tough terrain and with cattle. The Quarter horse is not only a working horse but has its own racing programme and is the fastest horse over a quarter of a mile. The breeds that you will see in the show ring are kept as true to the original working type as possible.

Having said all this, I am of the opinion that any horse can learn the work that we are covering in this book. It is true that he might not be able to perform it in the manner in which we may see the best working or competition horse do it, but that is not the point.

Temperament and aptitude

Whilst your horse might not be the 'ideal' shape there are two things that he most definitely can share with the purpose-bred horse and without these two requisites life can be a little difficult, but not impossible, for any horse. They are temperament and an aptitude to learn, although I feel that even an excitable horse could come to this work and benefit from it.

Remember that if your horse is finding something difficult and is getting upset or cannot go in the manner required then you should change the way you are asking or be prepared to compromise if necessary. This will take the pressure off your horse. As in all training, it is a case of having a lot of patience and time. He could end up surprising you, equally so you could surprise him! It is all about enjoying working together. You have already increased your horse's aptitude for work by going through the work in the other chapters including the voice training and this part never ceases as you can carry on building up the vocabulary.

Movement and your horse's size

I tend to work on the assumption that horses can do anything but as with people they may have some limitations. With the exception of three horses in training at the time of writing the rest are not the classical Western types, they range from cobby ponies to leggy 17hh Hanoverians with very expressive action. These horses are not for competition but for pleasure riding, teaching

Idolo, me and my old friend Boots.

and demonstrations. I take care to explain the differences in what I am showing if my horse is not going in 'competition' manner, which does happen sometimes.

If your horse has a low way of going, in other words there is not a lot of knee or shoulder movement and his feet stay close to the ground when going through the gaits, you are lucky. I do think that this is the easiest type of action to bring into Western mode. If, on the other hand, there is a lot of movement it will take a bit

longer, but it is not impossible, to train him to shorten his stride and this is covered in lesson 25.

We have one 11hh pony who is learning the work at the moment. He does voice training and long reining with the rider's mother – the rider is two years old! At the other extreme I have seen a shire horse out hacking in Western tack.

LESSON 22

WHAT IS NEEDED TO GET STARTED?

CLOTHING

I am sure that you have seen some pretty amazing costumes in books and magazines and there are different types of clothing to wear depending on what you actually want to do.

I tend to wear the most basic attire such as jeans and I often wear chaps and jodhpur boots. There are now more specialised Western shops which offer the full clothing range including boots. Whilst these are not essential when starting out you do need them if you wish to compete. I actually bought my first pair in a fashion shop! As with English riding it is not safe to ride in trainers or shoes with no heels. Chaps are useful and were designed to keep the cowboy warm, dry and to protect his legs against any sharp objects such as thorns and barbed wire. The long fringing seen on some chaps is not just for show but to help drain the water away. Some riders have said that they find that chaps help to stabilise them in the saddle, maybe it is the leather to leather, but I would not consider them a necessity.

The subject of hats is always open to discussion. Part of the accepted clothing is a stetson hat. This is soft and high enough to let the air circulate and has a brim to keep the sun off but really it would be of no use at all if you parted company with your horse. For adults with their own horses knowing all the risks the choice is theirs, however I would definitely suggest that novice or younger riders wear proper standard riding hats even on their own horses.

WHIPS AND SPURS

Spurs are part of the dress and the Western name for the whip is the 'quirt'. In any type of riding I very rarely carry a whip or wear spurs and to my knowledge they are not compulsory in Western competition but everyone I have seen wears them in the ring. I am of the opinion that an inexperienced rider should not wear them, too often spurs are used as a punishment instead of simply getting the horse lighter on the aid, if that is what is required.

THE BRIDLE AND BITS

In contrast to the English bridle which has as standard a browband, throat lash and noseband

there are a variety of types of bridle. Some have no browbands or throat lashes but just a split or a loop in the headstall for one ear to go through, these are often used when showing as the horse's head is then presented so that the bridle does not detract.

Many people look at the Western bit almost in horror. Yes, the horses are normally worked in curb bits but this is when they have finished their training, contrary to some other disciplines where the stronger bit goes in when the rider cannot control their horse. An interesting comparison would be that of advanced dressage, horses are required to go in a double bridle including a noseband. The finished Western horse in competition will go in a curb bit to show how light and responsive he is but nosebands are not allowed. If the horse opens his mouth at any time, this shows a lack of trust in the rider's hands, he may be frightened of the bit so the rider loses points. Basically if the horse has been trained correctly through the stages then the move into the curb will help to bring him into the final stages of lightness and softness. I think it might be interesting to have classes where horses actually work at the highest levels with the least amount of bitting and without the rider wearing spurs or carrying whips.

Most horses are started off in the bosal which is the true hackamore. It is a very thick rounded type of noseband that can be shaped to fit the horse's nose, it joins under the chin with the reins coming from that point. The pressure is applied to the front of the nose when the reins are used. It has a very different action to that of the mechanical hackamore, which is the one we are more familiar with as it is often seen in the showjumping ring. Some riders mistakenly think that this is softer on the horse than a bit. But the pressure placed on both the nose and the poll is very strong if applied by inexperienced hands.

I tend to be realistic when working with horses which are older and may have had a lot happening to their mouths over the years, sometimes they are so dead and dry in the mouth that both horse and rider are going downhill because of it. Never think of the bit as your brakes, your horse must be happy with it. One of my top horses had a very badly damaged mouth before I had him, he did not like the snaffle bit but he loved the pelham and I would only work him in a double at the shows. I try different bits to encourage the horse to mouth after checking out that there is no obvious reason for the problem. Just as we all have different jaw and teeth structures, so do horses. Some even have a tongue which is too big so they have to be bitted very carefully or not have a bit at all. If you are not interested in competing then you can use whatever bit your horse goes comfortably in. There is, however, a variety of Western snaffle bits available that you may find your horse would take to, such as the shanked snaffle which is jointed. Some of these have a small roller in the centre which stops the bit having the full nutcracker action for which snaffles are known. I consider these to be a stepping stone up to a curb bit.

Some bits are made with a metal other than stainless steel, these encourage the horse to enjoy the taste and the feel of the bit which will help if he has a dry mouth. If he has any problems in this area changing bits should help him to have a wet mouth. The ones I have seen have a copper inlay or a sweet-iron mouthpiece, mind you the sweet iron does not look very tasty as they are almost black and rusty to look at. Amongst those also used are the D-ring, loose ring and eggbutt snaffle which are also used in English riding.

The curb bit is only used when your horse has finished his training, in other words he is doing

everything as well as possible in the snaffle. But if your horse is happy in the bit you are training him in, whatever it is, unless you are going to compete, then I suggest you leave him in it. Whilst the curb bit does look strong with the long shanks and the ports my feelings are that, as with any bit, the horse's mouth will only be abused if the rider has bad hands. You may find it is worth talking to a good Western trainer or retailer regarding the type of tack available.

THE WESTERN SADDLE

There are different types of saddle to use depending on the work you wish to do, the important thing is that it fits correctly. I am sure you have seen some pictures of very ornate saddles, covered in silverware with a lot of tooling (hand carving on the leather) – these saddles are strictly for parades!

In comparison to the English saddles these do feel heavy; they were made to last for the cowboys but more importantly they spread the weight very evenly across the horse's back. A lot of them still have wooden trees but some are now made from fibreglass. As with English saddles you will find that there are different types for the work you want to do.

There are two main types of Western saddle: the working saddle and the pleasure (general purpose) saddle. Working saddles are sub-divided into cutting and roping saddles. Whilst these saddles have the same parts they are shaped to suit the rider and the way the rider is positioned in the saddle.

The parts that can differ most, depending on a rider's requirements, are: horns (high or low); swells (wide or narrow); seats (deep or shallow, sloped or flat, padded or hard); cantles (high or low); stirrups (wide or narrow treads).

Working saddles also have leather strings on them for tying on extra gear and packs. These strings may also appear on pleasure saddles but they are more likely to be purely decorative in this case.

When buying a Western saddle, the amount of tooling and/or silverware you have on it is a matter of personal choice but plain leather saddles are available if preferred.

Finally for those who do not want a leather saddle for whatever reasons there are synthetic Western saddles now available. As well as having the bonus of being very easy to clean, they are amazingly light to handle and put on the horse. Again, I would advise talking to someone who knows about Western tack to make sure you have the correct one for your purpose.

SADDLE PADS

Even though most of the saddles are lined underneath with imitation sheepskin, you must also use a good saddle pad. It is important that you use the pads and blankets that are designed for the job, either a one-piece blanket pad which is about one inch (2.5cm) thick or a pad which is about three-quarters of an inch (1.9cm) thick with a blanket on top.

LESSON 23

PARTS OF THE WESTERN TACK

THE BRIDLE

There are different types of Western bridles and in some competitions the type you use is important. The slot- or split-eared bridle (with the headstall designed with the split built into it) and the one-eared bridle (with a loop on the headstall) work on the same principle which is that the horse only has one ear through the bridle. Another type has a regular browband. On the whole these bridles do not have a throat lash, and nosebands do not feature.

THE REINS

With Western riding there are two types of reins, split or closed. Even though the final aim is to be able to neck rein your horse with one hand, and both types of reins can be used for this way of riding, schooling is often done with two hands so the split reins, I feel, are the best ones for this work.

Split or Texas reins are just two lengths of leather from six to seven feet (1.9 to 2.1m)

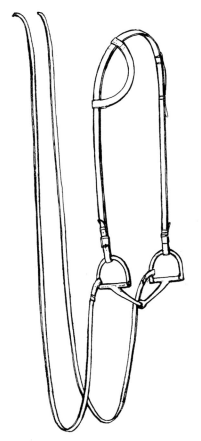

A basic western bridle: one eared, ringed snaffle and split reins.

long. They are attached to the bit but, as suggested by the name, they are not joined together and this allows the rider to ground-tie his horse without the risk of his getting his legs caught. I ride with the split rein but it is no use just undoing an English pair because they are not long enough. I sometimes use very long lead ropes if I am playing around and just working a horse in a headcollar but if you have small hands they might feel cumbersome.

Californian closed reins are joined together like the English reins but there is an extra piece added on called a roman or popper and this is used as a quirt, the equivalent to a whip. If you watch any competition you may see the reins seemingly so loose that you wonder why they are on at all. In fact this type of rein is made in such a manner that it is heavy so there is still contact with the mouth.

PARTS OF THE WESTERN SADDLE

Starting at the top and working down the parts are as described overleaf; the use of them will be explained in more detail when we fit the saddle.

The horn The horn is connected to the fork or swell, which is in front of the seat. Directly underneath this going down the centre of the saddle under the seat is the gullet. Around the back of the seat is the cantle.

The seat jockey Moving down, the piece coming off the seat on the sides is the seat jockey. To the front and below the swell on the seat jockey is the latigo holder.

The fenders These are the large pieces of leather which cover the stirrup leathers and they are connected to the saddle under the seat jockey and hold the stirrups. You will also find most stirrups have a hobble strap which goes around the bottom of the fender just above the stirrup. There are different types of stirrups depending on the work you wish to do.

The back jockey This is not on all saddles but when it is, it goes around the back end of the saddle behind the cantle and on top of the skirt. You may find saddle strings on both sides of the back jockey up near the cantle.

The rigging dee rings Underneath the seat jockey towards the front on the nearside you will find the front rigging dee ring. Joined onto this is the latigo.

On the offside you also have a front rigging dee and connected to this is the billet. Underneath the back jockey you will find the rear rigging dees, connected to these on both sides are the billets.

The latigo The latigo is a long strap about five feet (1.5m) in length and about three inches (7.6cm) wide joined to the nearside front rigging dee ring – it is equivalent to the girth strap on the English saddle. It connects the front cinch to the saddle.

The Western cinch, or girth I use a cinch that has a buckle at each end, on the offside the front cinch is buckled onto the billet. On the nearside it is connected to the saddle by the latigo. It is important that the buckles do not lie directly on the horse's skin, an extended piece from the cinch should come up behind them to protect the horse.

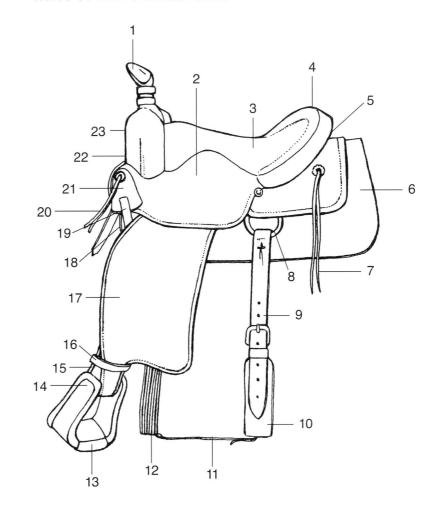

1 Horn
2 Seat jockey
3 Seat
4 Cantle
5 Back jockey
6 Skirt
7 Saddle strings
8 Rear rigging dee
9 Billet
10 Back cinch
11 Cinch connecting strap
12 Front cinch
13 Stirrup heel
14 Stirrup
15 Stirrup leather
16 Hobble strap
17 Fender
18 Front rigging dee
19 Latigo
20 String tie
21 Latigo holder
22 Gullet
23 Fork or swell

Parts of the Western saddle

The back or flank cinch The back or flank cinch provides stability to the saddle when used for roping. The action caused by the pressure on the rope when it is wrapped around the horn and being used to bring a steer down would tip the saddle up. You may even see trick riders using a back cinch for the same reasons – to keep the stability of the saddle when they are working over and around it.

I had a sharp reminder one day of the dangers involved when I put the back cinch on Hans when he had not worn it for a while. I mounted and he was fine but as I opened the gate and went through he just brushed it with his side. Normally it would not have bothered him but this time he blew his tummy out and even though the cinch was not tight, he came into contact with it. We finished the exercise

Note that the back cinch has some space between it and Hans' tummy. This is deliberate and it was during my chat that I saw the wheel was flat on the tractor!

turbo-charged! His four feet barely touching the ground, his head went down and his back came up. As well as running through all the words that I thought he would listen to I just kept him going around in a small circle. My prayers were answered; when we stopped I dismounted and then lunged him for a while!

The skirt This goes around the saddle and extends below the jockey.

LESSON 24

TACK FITTING AND TACKING UP

THE BRIDLE

Whichever headstall you are using (browband or one ear) be careful that your horse's ears are not pinched as obviously this will be very uncomfortable and might cause him to shake his head. The bit should lie in his mouth without causing the sides to wrinkle up. Much will depend on your horse's shape and size of mouth and the type of bit. How the bit lies in your horse's mouth also depends on many things, such as whether it is a straight bar or jointed bit, and the size of your horse's mouth. The bit must have contact with the corners of the mouth consequently this will create a slight creasing in the corners. Some bits are difficult to fit, such as a thick snaffle; the bit must also be the correct width and if you are not sure ask someone to check for you.

WHERE TO PUT THE REINS

I do not leave horses loose in their stables with a saddle or bridle on as there is a strong possibility that he could get the bridle caught on something. Most of my reins have hooks on them so I just take them off and put them on when needed; if you have fixed split reins place each one over the neck. If there is a throat lash I catch the reins up under this as well. I find that because of the length of the reins and having the horse tied he cannot put his head down so they tend not to slip. With joined reins I would hook them over the horn so they do not slip and use the throat lash if there is one.

FITTING THE WESTERN SADDLE

As with an English saddle, the Western one must fit correctly and you should try it without a pad. Whichever design of saddle you use, it must fit at the withers and have enough airspace through the gullet to stay clear of the back even with a rider on. If any part of the gullet touches the horse's spine, is tight on the withers or digs into any part of the back then the saddle is not right. If you are not sure, it is worth getting an experienced person to check this over for you.

SETTING THE FENDERS

One comment I have heard from riders before now is that they were uncomfortable and that their ankles ached. This was caused by fighting against the angle of the stirrup because the fenders had not been set. If you stand in front of the saddle and the stirrups are hanging parallel to the horse's sides or when you are sitting on the horse you find that you need to turn your toes in to place your feet into the stirrups and it is a fight to keep your toes facing straight ahead, then it sounds as if the fenders need setting. To do this oil them lightly, then soak the back of the fenders and stirrup leathers with water. Put the saddle down flat on the floor with the fenders and stirrup leathers out to each side, then take the stirrup and bend it over so that you get a diagonal crease down the fender. Place a good size weight on the top of each one and by doing this the leather stretches then sets. This way the stirrups are more comfortable to use, and do not break your ankles! Another way to set the fenders is to oil and soak as before then put the saddle onto a rack, put the stirrups into the position you want them, then place a broom handle through both and secure them. Leave them until they are set into the position you want.

BEFORE SADDLING

As you will see, the Western saddle is quite different from an English one; apart from the weight it is bigger to look at. You might think this odd but when the horse is having the saddle put on for the first time or two I leave the saddle on the door so that my horse can look at it and smell it but not eat it! With the horse tied up, I carry the saddle around the stable, particularly if he is a horse that tends to be a little nervous. For the first saddling I would have someone else around just in case I needed them to stand at my horse's head talking to him and stroking him.

HOW TO PUT THE SADDLE ON

It is your decision whether you put the bridle or saddle on first. Even though my horse will stand still while I tack him up, I do put the headcollar on as a matter of course. I do this for safety and also because it is good for them to wait while tied and tacked up – it is all part of their training.

Firstly put on the saddle pad and place it up over the withers, this way you can then slide it back with the saddle on into the correct position. Whatever weight your saddle is do not throw it onto your horse's back as seen in films, not only will this frighten him but it could bruise his back.

Before you even move the saddle, do secure all the hanging parts so they do not get tangled up with you when handling the saddle. Place the latigo out of your way, loop it over the horn or thread it through the dee ring. Either disconnect the cinch totally or place it over the seat. I also tend to hook the offside stirrup over the horn, this way it lessens the lifting height and there is no chance of the stirrup getting caught between the saddle and the horse.

I have one horse who is quite tall and I can tell you it is impossible for me to put my Western saddle on from the floor, so I use a safe wooden block to stand on and I suggest you do the same if you feel the need to – it does make life much

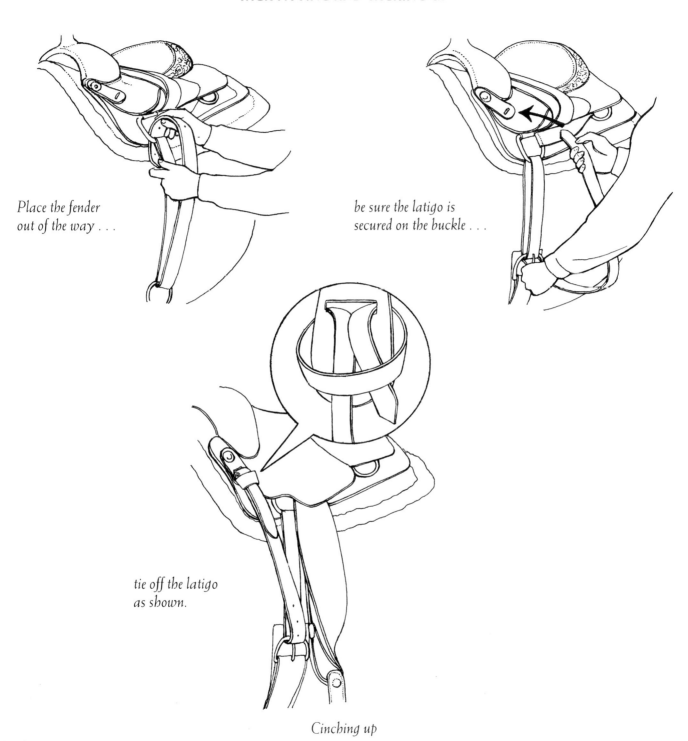

Place the fender
out of the way . . .

be sure the latigo is
secured on the buckle . . .

tie off the latigo
as shown.

Cinching up

easier! Remember to keep talking to your horse while you are working around him and definitely when lifting the saddle up and gently placing it down onto the pad. Make sure there is at least two inches (5cm) of pad showing at the front. Carefully slide the pad and saddle back into the correct position, and when it is in place lift up your saddle a little by the horn and make sure the pad fits into the gullet. If you do not do this, a lot of pressure will go onto the withers and spine when you sit into the saddle and your horse could get serious pressure problems, as well as pain. It is very important to double check this, particularly if you did not saddle up yourself.

CINCHING UP

Arrange the cinch so that the buckles will be evenly balanced on each side of your horse. Undo the latigo making sure it is not twisted; due to the length I would expect to do two wraps. Bring the latigo through the cinch buckle from the inside to the outside (towards you) then take it up to the dee ring and, putting it through, pull it down to the buckle again. When you do this make sure that it lies underneath the first wrap so that it does not pinch the horse's skin, and then bring it through the buckle again. This type of girth is very easy to do up too tightly, so be careful of this when taking up the slack. If you are happy with the feel when you put your hand between the latigo and your horse's rib cage then put the buckle tongue in the hole. Take the spare latigo up, thread it through the latigo carrier from the outside to the inside and pull it down so that it lies flat. If you still have spare over then tie it off in a special knot as I will describe. Take the spare latigo which is hanging down with your left hand across to the right. Then thread it up through the dee ring but from the inside to the outside, now thread the spare latigo down through the piece that goes across it and let it hang down. I then pull my horse's knees forward to make sure that the skin is smooth under the cinch.

If you have a back cinch, it must be done up loosely enough so that if your horse expands his stomach he does not feel it, also remember it must be connected to the front cinch. *Always* do it up last and undo it first. I cannot emphasise enough the importance of the back cinch being done up last and of being undone first. I once heard of someone who was busy talking to a friend while they were attending to their horse. Without thinking they undid the front cinch first, there was a commotion outside the stable which caused the horse to shoot sideways. It was pure chance they managed to catch the saddle before it slipped around the horse's side and maybe caused a bad accident.

LESSON 25

MOUNTING YOUR HORSE AND THE RIDER'S POSITION

DO YOU STRETCH?

So much time is spent thinking about what we are going to do with our horses or other things that have to be done, that it is very easy to forget about our bodies. No, I do not mean that you should be in the gym and start trying to build the body beautiful, you might have that already! But the fact is that as we get older our joints tend to tighten and stiffen so the flexibility is lost. Having said that, I have also known teenagers who would often complain of backache, therefore I think that rules out the possibility of problems just being age related!

For the youngsters it can be that once they have gone past the age when they have to do physical education at school, riding is their only hobby and all some professionals do is ride and stand giving lessons. If you have any aches or pains do think about them; there is a strong chance that, in an effort to protect that area when riding, some part of your body will try to help it out by tensing up. The more common problems which can affect the back in particular are tight hamstrings and soft stomach muscles. Whatever your age you should at least work on stretching and tightening, which can be done through what is called low impact exercise such as callinetics and yoga.

THE MOUNTING BLOCK

Whatever type of riding we do we always use a mounting block irrespective of the horse's age and size. Having said that, I must point out that all my horses can be mounted from the floor if needed. You also need to train your horse to stand next to odd-looking objects on which you can balance to mount from. Even if you only have one horse, think how many times you will mount him from the same side, putting the pressure on the same part of his back.

MOUNTING YOUR HORSE

There are two ways to mount, the traditional way facing your horse's rear or the one I tend to favour which is the one that most Western riders

use. I find that if the horse tries to walk away it is easier to stop him from this position which I will describe. Mount from either the floor or the block and make sure that your horse is standing square and tell him to stand up. Standing close to your horse in line with the saddle and facing slightly to the front, take the reins in your left hand so that you have a contact with your horse's mouth, split them with your index finger and place your hand on the withers.

At the same time that you put your right hand on either the offside swell or the horn, place your left foot in the stirrup. From this position you should be able to spring up and gently settle yourself into the saddle. As you are mounting, listen to your horse, watch his ears – is he with you or has his attention wandered elsewhere? Be ready to give a quick feel down the rein if you feel he is going to move, at the same time tell him to stand still.

When you first start riding Western you will need to make a very conscious effort as you are mounting your horse to be aware of where your right leg goes and give the cantle plenty of clearance.

BEFORE MOVING-OFF

As a matter of course after I am settled in the saddle I say 'good boy', give my horse a piece of carrot (this is good for stretching his neck) and a pat on the neck. Then I wait for a couple of minutes before we move off. Horses are creatures of habit so it is well worth taking the time to do this, then he will learn not to move off as soon as I am in the saddle. Otherwise this could build up into not wanting to stand still at all. If he starts to move I feel down both reins and close the knees, as this is my downward transitions aid. I also give the verbal aid 'stand'. As he responds I ease the contact a touch so he feels the difference and I immediately praise him.

Possible problem and correction

I have included this piece because having your horse stand still when mounting really is the most important lesson he needs to learn and understand. Equally so it is your responsibility to show and teach him what is wanted. We had one horse who came to us because he had got into the habit of bolting as the rider was just getting up from the floor, obviously this was highly dangerous for both of them. The horse was an ex-racehorse but the new owner did not realise that the majority of trainers have the lads legged-up while the horse is walking around. It was possible therefore that previously the horse had not learnt to stand still and be mounted from the floor. So now he was panicking because of the toe tickling him behind the elbow, the pull on the saddle and then the contact with the reins. Looking at it like this, from the horse's point of view, helps you to assess the problem and how to go about helping the horse to adjust to this new movement. It also helps the rider to rethink how to make what they were about to do a pleasant experience for the horse.

For us it was a case of taking the horse back to square one, using the ever ready hip bag full of goodies, plus a lot of verbal praise. He went back on the lunge with tack on for a short while to

(Opposite) We always mount from a raised area of some description, hence the straw bale. The rider here is giving the cantle plenty of clearance which is good.

establish the words and start to respond to them. He was handled a lot all over, I would push into the sensitive areas and encourage him to take the pressure without running away from it, giving much praise at the same time. The aim was to desensitise him, particularly in the area the foot would be touching. The saddle was moved around and banged and all the time I was talking and patting him. When I had finished and he had accepted what I had done he was given more praise and some food. He learnt to associate what I was doing with treats.

For the actual getting on him, I put him in an area where he faced towards something solid so there was no obvious exit point and with someone at his head with a lunge. Keeping an even contact on the reins I practised getting on from a block but just balancing on the stirrup. Over time, as he gained confidence in me, I did get into the saddle from where he got plenty of pats and food from me. Because his owner was quite short and not very agile I advised them never to try and mount from the ground as this could cause the problem to return but not through any real fault of theirs or of the horse's.

THE WESTERN POSITION

On the whole I find the saddle tends to put you into the correct position. As you settle into the seat think about your seat bones and your pelvis should be neither tipped backwards nor forwards. I think of sitting squarely with the weight evenly distributed through my seat, the only times I alter the weight in my seat is when I want my horse to do a downward transition, then I think of making the back of my seat heavier. Your head should be up and looking straight ahead, if you look down you automatically put more weight down your front and lighten your seat, so you will give your horse confusing aids.

The aim is to have your shoulders, hips and heels in line with a slight bend in the knees, rather the same as when riding English-style. You should think of sitting tall in the saddle without tension, that can be easy to say but not always so easy to do! So you need to practise isolating, tightening and releasing your muscles, remember each part of you should be able to move independently as needed without interfering with other parts but the aim is that it all works together as one.

HAND POSITION WITH ONE AND TWO REINS

When riding with two hands, your arm position is the same as in English riding. There should be a straight line from your elbow down to your hands with no tension with your fingers ready to talk down the reins to your horse's mouth. Cross the reins over the neck so they hang down each side, carry your hands in front of the horn, above the withers and about six to ten inches (15 to 25cm) apart. Hold both reins in your hands and they will now form what we call a bridge over the withers. It is up to you whether you leave your little finger inside the reins or if you put it outside and have the reins coming between the fourth finger and the little finger.

To ride with one hand, use whichever hand is comfortable. Closed reins come up through the bottom of your hand and out of the top, you close your fingers around the reins. The romal

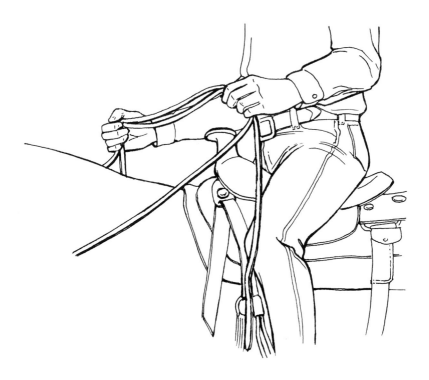

This is a bridged rein. The space may well vary between the hands in individual riders. The latigo has not been tied off here.

should then be carried in the other hand which rests on your thigh. With split reins, place your index finger between them and turn your hand so that the thumb is uppermost. The reins should now hang down through the hand, with the spare length of rein lying down your horse's shoulder on the same side as the controlling (left) hand, i.e. the nearside shoulder. To be technically correct if you wished to compete, your other arm should be carried with a slight bend in the elbow, not resting or touching any part of your body. However we need to be realistic and this would get very tiring, so when I am just out riding I do rest my hand on my thigh.

POSITION AWARENESS

It can be very easy to get into bad habits if you work on your own so you must always think about what your body is doing, particularly if you are starting this work. Sometimes if the horse is having trouble understanding the rider's request, the rider starts to do odd things with their body in an effort to help the horse. You must be very aware of this happening, because it can actually interfere not help. The other time problems can crop up is when the rider becomes so involved with what the horse is doing they forget about themselves, again they might twist or lean over but without realising it.

The riding position is very important because it can help or hinder the horse. All too often one sees a really good horse working in any discipline, then you look at the rider and wonder why they do not realise they are sitting incorrectly. Thinking riding is not difficult, you just have to make yourself aware of what you are doing and what is happening to you and your horse. If there is a problem give your horse a breather while you analyse it. The essence of being a real rider and trainer is knowing that less is more, and knowing when to accept what is being offered or when to ask and to encourage your horse for that bit extra.

I can think of nothing better to watch than a horse and rider working together as a pair, almost reading each other's minds. The rider quiet and still in the saddle with nothing appearing to be asked, yet the horse ready but relaxed and offering his all. That is real horsemanship.

LESSON 26

THE GAITS

THE GAITS

This word covers the walk, trot, canter and gallop. Each of these gaits has different beats and rhythm; I will explain in the next chapter how you achieve these gaits. Out of the gaits we are covering the two that are specific to Western are the jog and the lope. It is actually possible to do things but not always realise the breakdown of how they work, which is why I felt it would be useful to include the following sections.

Walk

This is a four-beat gait, I say 'beat' because the horse moves his feet in four separate beats. So the sequence of the walk is as follows: off hind, off fore, near hind and lastly near fore. The most important aspect of the walk is the rhythm which must be a very clear four-beat, anything else is incorrect. So do practise watching your horse walking on the lunge, set your eye on the off hind and then count the steps one-two-three-four.

Also, when riding try to feel when each leg is being lifted. By developing your feel you will also realise quickly if your horse starts to walk short or takes a short stride particularly with a hind leg. By homing in on your feel and sharpening it up, you will also be able to tell if your horse needs more activity, impulsion or even to shorten the strides more.

Pacing, an incorrect walk
Sometimes you may see a horse walking but it does not look right in as much as the outside hind and outside foreleg move forward at the same time, followed by the inside hind with the inside foreleg, in other words the pairs are moving laterally. The walk has now become two-beat or the pace and is incorrect, (in fact this is how camels move, not that this is a comparison to your horse but a factual observation). If you are not sure about your horse's pace when riding him, one of the tell-tale signs is that the pace has a left to right rolling lilt to it.

Trot

The trot is a two-beat gait but is not the same as pacing – the trot pairs move diagonally. The inside hind and outside fore move together as one pair and while these are moving forward in

Floribunda is jogging here. Note how the hind legs are undertracking, in other words not stepping into or over the prints left by the front feet, and this is correct.

the air, the outside hind with the inside foreleg are on the ground. The movement is repeated, giving you the one-two beat, and propels the horse forward. This is why when the rider first starts to learn to post or rise to the trot they have difficulty getting into an 'up down' rhythm. Whilst in Western riding the full range of trots that are used in dressage are not required, for the working trot your horse should still track up. In other words, when trotting, the hind foot should at least go into the hoof print left by the front foot.

Jog
The jog is still a diagonal two-beat gait but it is a slower and shorter striding gait than the trot. In

comparison to the working trot, in the jog the horse will undertrack by quite a few inches, that is the hind feet land short of the tracks left by the front feet. It is very comfortable for this reason and because there is less movement. When the jog is being ridden, it is still of the utmost importance that the strides are a clear two-beat rhythm, the horse should not drag his toes along the ground, nor should it look as if he is doing a fast walk.

Canter

The canter is a three-beat gait and he will canter either with the left lead or the right lead. The sequence of canter when you are on the left leg is as follows: the off hind pushes and starts the stride, following by the diagonal pair of the near hind and off fore together. Finishing the stride is the near fore which makes it the left-lead canter. The sequence for the right lead is as follows: near hind pushes off to start the stride, then the off hind and near fore together, finishing with the off fore as the lead leg. This gives you a regular one-two-three beat and rhythm.

It is important that the horse is balanced in the canter. Going straight he can easily pick up on either lead leg without feeling unbalanced but if you always let him canter on whichever leg he wants, then you may well find that he will favour one leg. Your horse will then get a muscular build up for the lead he favours and in turn will become stiff and unbalanced and will possibly then have difficulty getting onto the other lead when asked. You need, therefore, to be aware of which leg your horse is cantering on when you are out working him or even just riding out. I make a habit of asking for whichever lead I would like my horse to go off on.

Lope

The lope is a slow canter with the stride shortened. Even though it is a three-beat gait the rhythm is altered slightly and the strides are made slower. What happens is that the horse holds for a fraction longer on the first beat than on the next two beats, so instead of being one-two-three it becomes one pause, two-three. You must be very careful that he does not go into a four-time canter in your effort to slow him down. This will happen if you break the sequence of the second beat which is the diagonal pair.

Gallop

In beat terms the gallop is not just a speeded up canter, it has a very definite four-beat rhythm. The sequence is as follows: to start the stride, the pushing leg is the outside hind, then the inside hind, then the outside fore and finally the inside fore. You can see that this sequence has come about because the second beat in the canter, the diagonal pair has been broken so giving us the extra beat.

The gallop is not used in Western competition, except maybe in the rundown to a sliding stop, which I hasten to add we will not be covering in this book – that's well past just getting started!

LESSON 27

THE BASICS OF WESTERN RIDING

BEFORE ANYTHING

If neither you nor your horse have worked Western before then treat it as if you are starting out on an adventure. You are going on a new path with only a map, it is possible you might take a wrong turning and not end up where you are aiming for. If this happens you will have to retrace your steps. The same applies to your horse, work logically, be very careful not to create problems or ask him to do something that he is not ready for. If there is a problem go back, think about it and start again. It is your responsibility to make it so easy that he cannot misunderstand. The idea is that you present him with what you are asking him to do in such a manner that he just goes with the flow. It should not be presented as anything difficult although it is new. It is easy to try too hard and want too much – beware!

With any animal, you are always striving to build a partnership, co-operating with each other and building solid foundations for your work, in fact all of this is relevant to whatever work you are doing with your horse.

THE WAY OF GOING

We have covered the gaits, the position and mounting your horse. Now, whether you wish to compete or simply ride for pleasure, it is important that I make you aware of the correct way of going for the Western horse. The majority of riders who ride English will ride their horse with a contact down the rein to the mouth. If you are a schooling rider you most probably will have your horse working up and in self-carriage. As we are not going out to find a horse bred for the job, it is possible that your horse might not be able to go in quite the manner that is sought after for showing. Do not let this put you off, as I have said earlier be prepared to come to an agreement and work out a happy medium.

THE BASICS

Going back to 'the more the horse knows from the ground the better', do take time to cover the sections relevant to the moving from pressure and getting him on the verbal aids. Both of you

will need to have an understanding from the ground before you progress to asking for sideways work from the saddle, this will make everything much easier for both of you.

I work on the theory that you should be able to bend the neck left or right without the rest of the body following, you aim to be able to move the neck and shoulders over and finally you should be able to move the quarters without the rest of the body following. By being able to move each part of your horse you can then work the whole of him together as one. An exercise I do is slowly bending my horse's neck to the left then to the right at the halt, walk, trot and canter. The important part to this being that only the head and neck move off the line I am taking so I know that my horse is balanced and supple. You should be able to do this if you take your time stretching him, which you can also do in the stable, and through working your horse in the correct manner.

Often people say that they cannot work their horse through the winter because of the lack of light so the horse suffers from a lack of work as he is only put out in the field. Remember that you can do many exercises with your horse in the stable to stop him stiffening and tightening up, particularly if he is an older horse. Also good grooming stimulates the muscles.

We have covered the things you need to know from the tack to mounting your horse, now we work on how to train your horse into this new way of going and working with you.

I am asking Hans to bend round to the right at the halt. While asking with the right rein I am very clearly allowing with the left. This exercise can progress in all the gaits, but be very aware of the horses body staying straight when using forward movement.

ON THE BIT

For me this means the horse is accepting the bit with a relaxed jaw and giving over the poll area, by doing this he will have his nose either on or near the vertical. In turn when he is on the bit you will find that he can flex or bend more easily when asked. The difference between English and Western on this matter is that there is little or no rein contact in Western but the horse should still carry the bridle in the correct manner.

If you have worked through the previous chapters following the long reining and lungeing your horse should be working on the bit. In case you cannot quite get it, try the following method. Remember you are aiming to get him working with the loose contact, so you need to really show him what you are after and make it easy for him to understand. Have your horse standing at the halt, sit squarely in the saddle with your legs on his sides. Have the reins bridged across the withers, keep a steady contact on one rein and feel the other one by opening and closing the fingers. As he starts to relax his jaw, give him plenty of praise. Then stop working the fingers and ease the rein forward. If he goes to put his nose forward again, quietly repeat the process then stop and use the fingers on the other rein but do not saw the mouth, in other words alternate left, right, left. 'Talk' down the rein when your horse is against the hand, say 'no' and apply soft pressure, but when he responds cease and say 'good boy' – that is his reward for answering the question. He will start to realise that when his nose is forward something happens to his mouth but when he relaxes, it stops and is quiet. You should be able to feed the reins out slowly and get them to the length you want to work with. Always make a

fuss of him verbally and give plenty of pats.

Doing this at the halt gives both of you time to work out what is happening. When making any transition I do actually feel the rein to make sure my horse knows where I want him to stay with his head, if I feel a problem happening. When moving I also use my legs with equal pressure during this transition in conjunction with my rein and voice aids.

THE OUTLINE

In Western riding the outline required from your horse is different. We are looking for him to carry his head and neck in such a manner that his eyes are roughly level with his wither height, and his jaw should be relaxed and accepting the bit. Whilst the neck is lower than you are most probably used to, do not confuse this with being on the forehand. Your horse should never be heavy and leaning on the hand, he must carry himself and have his quarters under him so that he can carry out the work that is being asked of him.

Your aim should be to encourage your horse to work on a contact that is soft and as light in the hand as is possible. That does not mean that you ride with your fingertips barely holding the reins, the soft hand holds the rein well in the hand with the fingers closed. Beware that the reins do not get short and tight, you are aiming to ride with them longer than you are maybe used to. When needed, use your fingers to talk down the reins to the horse's mouth.

I have explained about the way your horse should go but more importantly you are the one who will ask and influence his way of going. It is very easy to say he won't do this or do that; very

rarely will a horse say 'no', if he does, he is probably being asked in a manner that he does not understand or he is not yet able to do something.

Being a considerate and sensitive rider with good soft hands does not mean that the horse is allowed to do what he wants but that the rider has the ability and knowledge to make a correction immediately it is required so that the horse understands what the correction is for. The other important factor is that the rider does not 'make a mountain out of a molehill' but carries on in a relaxed manner so that both of them think forward to the next bit of work and not about what has happened.

YOUR POSITION AND ITS INFLUENCE

We covered your position earlier, now we need to discuss how to use it to your best advantage. As with your horse, you need to be able to use every part of your body individually but be able to work it all together when required. Do practise isolating different groups of muscles, feel how they affect you when you tighten them up, then compare the difference when you release them. The parts to use are the voice which is used in all sections of this book, throughout the training programme, the legs, hands, seat and your brain.

The seat

Using your seat and how you distribute your weight through it plays an important part in Western riding, however you must understand how to use it without collapsing your hips and shoulders or rounding the lower back. To help give you an idea of the feel, I would like you to sit on a hard chair. Place your hands underneath your seat and you will feel your seat bones. Be aware of what your body is doing, in other words do not let any part collapse while practising these exercises. Try putting more pressure down into one seat bone then the other, you should feel this on the relevant hand as you do it. By doing this when riding you should be able to move your horse sideways away from the pressure. By putting the weight down into both seat bones your horse will learn this is for the downward transitions, I also close my knees on the saddle in conjunction with the seat and voice.

Also, try doing the exercise incorrectly on one occasion. Put a lot of weight on one seat bone, really pushing, and drop the shoulder down towards the hip, this way you learn the feel of when it is wrong.

Sometimes when trying too hard the rider tightens up the seat muscles and the lower back, this will then effectively push the seat out of the saddle. While you are riding around tighten your seat, you will feel how your whole body pops up, then when you relax you drop down again.

The legs

It is quite interesting, when I start working with new riders, finding out how they would like their horse to go; maybe they are having a few problems between them. A common comment that is made is that the horse does not move off the leg. I like my horses to move forward when I ask by closing my legs on his sides, as well as using my voice aid. I do not keep the pressure on, I ask and then release the pressure so my legs are on his sides ready to ask for something else. If I do not get a response when I ask I give a stronger voice aid and I will give a kick with

both legs but, very importantly, I allow him to move forward through the reins as he responds to my aid, then he is given praise for responding. This might sound rather sharp but it is not, my aid is then clear to my horse and he respects my leg.

Never kick and then stop him strongly with the reins, this is a total contradiction to what he is being asked to do, yet I have often seen people doing just this. One part is telling him to go and when he responds he suddenly gets hit in the mouth! That is such an illogical thing to do, no wonder the horse gets tense and worried. He answered the request, even if he was a little slow, then he feels pain in the mouth for doing what he was asked.

If you keep your legs on tightly all the time there is a strong chance that you will end up basically riding every stride from your horse. On the other hand if you keep nagging, scrubbing or kicking your horse's sides, you will find eventually that he will stop listening to your legs! For me the pleasure in riding is that my horse does the work, I ask and he responds.

My theory then is that your legs should be hanging down softly but on your horse's sides ready to give whatever aid is required. Do not make the mistake of getting your horse so sharp off the aid that your leg cannot move without him diving sideways, he should always wait for a positive request.

If your horse is very dead off the leg then you need to find out why. Perhaps it is your riding that has caused it, maybe your leg has continually kicked him on the side. Parts of our bodies do things to our horses without our knowledge! Examples of this are being heavy handed and giving him a dead mouth or sitting with more weight on one seat bone than the other, thereby making him adjust his balance to

carry us. He will feel straight to the rider but he is in fact moving crooked with his quarters slightly to the left or right. It could be that your horse has a general lethargy problem. If so it might be worth having him looked over by a vet or do a feeding check.

The hands and reins

I often tell people always to think of their hands and reins as only accessories and never to rely on them – you should be able to ride without them but you do need them for the training work! In the Western Pleasure class the reins are so slack they are looped, so you really must do the homework in training. I think you will find that all Western trainers do train two-handed no matter what level the horse is, as you do need to direct rein the aid for various exercises such as stretching and bending the horse. The one-hand working is for the finished horse in competition or if you are just wanting to hack.

The term 'neck reining' is used for when you are working one-handed and the horse moves from the pressure of the reins against the neck and it is called an 'indirect aid'. However, he is first taught to move away from pressure when ridden with two reins; holding the reins in two hands as explained, you then use them as directed. The indirect rein aid is given as follows: the outside rein is leant against the neck but do not take your hand over the neck, at the same time you feel on the inside rein; the direct rein aid gives your horse an indication of the direction you wish him to go in. As your horse responds, stop asking with the direct rein and just leave the indirect one against the neck.

As your horse becomes more responsive to the new aids and moves when asked, you can then progress to riding with one hand. When asking your horse to neck rein your hand should

stay over the withers, giving aids that are imperceptible to those watching but we need to be realistic and remember that you are starting out. So, you can either flex the wrist over to the left or right as needed, this will increase the pressure on the neck and your horse should move away from the pressure. Alternatively you can move the forearm either side of the neck; this would give your horse a more obvious aid but remember this is only a transitional phase.

A common mistake that is made by newcomers to the sport is that, when neck reining, the hand is brought over the neck in an effort to bring the horse round. This though will cause the horse to have the wrong bend, consequently he will fall in on the shoulder and corner rather like a motor bike which is totally incorrect.

The brain

This should be used when riding and I call it thinking riding. It is relevant to all types of riding. Mind you, in the nicest possible way I do ask some of my riders where theirs is at times! When I first take a rider, at whatever level they are, I say to them 'this may be different from what you are used to, I want you to tell me what is happening, what you are doing and what you are feeling'. By doing this I then find out how much they know and how their feel is developing. I do not want them relying on me to tell them what to do all the time, they must learn to follow their own instinct. Actually sometimes a rider will say it feels bad or wrong, but from the floor it looks fine and I will tell them, so they start to think about this new feeling and accept that it is correct. This is part of being a thinking rider, our lessons are interactive, talking and discussing about what is or is not happening. I feel this is the best way to learn, to be able to

retain something and then to put it into operation, particularly when they are working at home or at a show alone. If you are not sure what something looks like when riding get into the habit of checking the shadows when you can, this does help.

So get your brain into gear when you are going out to work your horse and have some plan as to the direction you will be working in but do not be rigid in your approach. While you are walking around think about the feel he is giving you; when working you might suddenly think 'this is good I wonder if I should try something else'. Do it, do not just think about it, you do need to stretch both of you to progress, and as long as you lead into it correctly it should be fine. In fact you will know that your training is working when you find that your horse offers something new.

Above all, remember you are seeking co-operation, not domination, with your horse. It is give and take for both of you.

THE DISMOUNT

I tend to dismount the traditional English way, which is to take both feet out of the stirrups, as I do feel that it is safer. Ride your horse forward into halt; use your voice aids as well. Standing him up squarely, sit and wait a minute before you dismount. Make sure that he is listening then put the reins into the left hand, place them on your horse's neck just in front of the withers. Be ready to give a quick feel down the reins and tell him to halt if you think he is about to try and walk on. Take both feet out of the stirrups, put the right hand on the swell then leaning forward slightly throw the right leg well over the cantle

and push off with the right hand. As you land bend your knees, so that you absorb some of the shock through them and not your back. Straighten and make much of your horse; if you have finished work then loosen off the cinch strap a few holes.

I have to admit there have been some very amusing instances that could have ended rather badly if the people had been on their own. Ironically in each of the following cases if the Western dismount (i.e. leaving the left foot in the stirrup until the right foot reaches the ground) had been used neither would have had a problem! I will pass both on to you because they may make it a case of 'rider beware of the clothes you wear when riding'. To set the scene, both women were riding big horses but it did not really matter what size they were, the outcome would have been the same I think. Fortunately for both women their horses stood like statues and did not move.

One friend suddenly needed to cut the lesson short to go to the bathroom and I stayed in the arena working my horse. As I passed the entrance I looked out to see her apparently dismounting but as I carried on watching she was stationary on the side of the horse but her feet were not touching the ground and she was making funny actions with her legs. As I made my way out to her I called and she replied 'I'm stuck.' I jumped off my horse got hold of hers while she endeavoured to get her arms out of the tee shirt she had been wearing. As she had dismounted her tee shirt had got hooked over the saddle horn and pulled her up short, her feet were hanging about one and half feet off the floor, due to the time hanging and the struggling the saddle had started to slip round. That was one very lucky person! She said that she had not called for help because she was not wearing a bra and did not fancy one of the lads giving her a hand. The other friend always threw her leg over the front of the saddle and would laugh when I put my hands over my eyes. One day she did that and went to slide down to the floor but the back of her coat got caught on the horn and she was stuck half way, luckily I managed to undo her coat because she could not move her arms to get loose.

LESSON 28

EXERCISES AND TRAIL WORK

Trail work can be compared to the English equivalent of handy pony classes. All the exercises described are relevant to both styles of riding as a form of training but some are specific to the Western horse. Much importance will be attached to his ability to perform the work, as it really could be a matter of life or death. That might sound dramatic but think about it. If you were chasing a steer through unknown territory in the mountains or going up a rough, narrow path that you found was blocked, then you would need to be able to rein back knowing that the horse would listen to your aids and not push back into your leg. If he did then you would be heading down the ravine in no uncertain manner. Your horse should be able to turn around on the spot without gaining an inch either backwards or forwards.

In this chapter we will cover simple exercises which if you want to just ride Western are useful and if you are aiming to compete are essential. The trail work is very good for all horses, not only Western ones. If you do not like jumping then these will work your horse and give him something else to learn. Also he will be using his body in a different manner to what he is used to, stimulating him both mentally and physically.

TRANSITIONS

If you cannot ride a transition then you are lost, because I think they and the half halt can make or break the way a horse works and lets you ride him. Anyone can sit on a horse and go around or ride out but even though to change from one gait to another is technically a transition, it really is about the manner in which it is performed by your horse that makes it. He can only do a good one if you have prepared him for it and not just pulled on the reins or let him flop into it. This is true of either the upward or the downward transitions.

I use the walk for my loosening up work and when training new movements I always establish them in the walk first, then move up a gear. When changing up from one gait to another, prepare him with a half halt so he does not alter or speed up the rhythm, then give him

the aids. If he lengthens, say 'no steady', half halt again and repeat the aids. On the downward changes again prepare him with the half halts to get him listening and lightening the front end so he does not go on the forehand when you give him the aids.

Try to keep all your aids easy for your horse to understand. Think of your seat and the weight distribution; to slow down or stop make your seat heavier depending on which of those two responses you are after. Then lighten it fractionally to move him forward within the gait but not when you are changing gaits as this will make him go faster which you do not want. Use different pressure from your knees, thighs or calves for the upward and downward transitions, it only needs to be a slight difference but he will learn and start to offer you what you want more quickly as he gets more sure and confident in his knowledge.

SETTING THE SPEED IN THE GAITS

One of the exercises I do when lungeing one of my horses in a roller and side-reins, is to ask him to slow the trot so that he is jogging and to shorten the steps from the full length stride. Do this by saying 'steady, slower' and feeling on the lunge at the same time. As he responds praise him with 'good boy' and keep repeating this until you get him working at the speed and in the rhythm you are looking for. When you want him to move forward again and lengthen the stride say 'all right, forward'. To make sure that he is using his hind legs properly also ask him to halt and rein back then move off again in a good clean transition. By doing this a few times you are ensuring that he is using his quarters and

carrying himself. It is important that he does not break the rhythm so be ready to ask him to move on. You can also do this on the long reins and this all helps the ridden work.

USING THE HALF HALT TO BALANCE

When riding, the main things you are looking for in any gait are the rhythm and balance. The horse should not be leaning on your hand and this is where the half halts help. With bridged reins when you have asked your horse to go into trot, go rising and let him establish the rhythm. Then think about moving him into the jog, go into sitting trot on a large circle, think about following the movement and not blocking it with your lower back and seat. Try not to use the rein as the main aid for shortening the stride, if you are not careful you can end up only slowing the trot and losing the impulsion in the back end.

To half halt I drop the weight into my seat, close my knees and give a feel on both reins for less than a stride and at the same time I say 'steady'. I immediately then ease the hands forward so that he does not lean on the reins but balances himself. By doing this I put a hesitation into the stride and effectively this puts the weight onto my horse's quarters thus lightening the forehand. I repeat this until I get my horse working in the speed and rhythm that I am after. Talk to him while you are asking for this work and use the voice to settle him if he starts to get worried by this new request. When your horse is learning make sure that you do not ask for too much, he is going to be using his muscles in a different way so they will get tired. To finish the movement either bring him into

walk or push him forward to trot and let him stretch.

To bring the canter into the lope you will use the same aids but the timing is different, it is best to half halt in the same manner as before but now you should try and do it when your horse's withers are lifting up. This would be just as the horse is going to complete the last sequence of the stride and by doing it at this point your horse will already have his quarters underneath him and you are encouraging him to 'sit' and again put the weight on to the hindquarters. This puts the hesitation into the stride and helps you to shorten him up. Practice is the only way in all of this work that you and your horse will progress. Do a few short strides then ease him forward to relax and reward him.

THE FIRST MOVEMENT

After you have mounted and settled into the saddle, sit up but without being tense in your body. The first movement you will do is ask your horse to move off walking forward actively in a straight line. Prepare him by asking him to give his jaw and be on the bit, as he relaxes allow the contact to ease before you ask him to move off. When you are ready ask him to 'walk on' and at the same time close your legs and allow with your hands. As he responds, ease your leg aid and praise him. Make sure the pressure is equal from your legs otherwise he may well go sideways. As he is walking feel the movement and let your seat follow it. Think about how your lower back is moving, do not exaggerate following the walk, just go with the flow.

Possible problem
It is quite normal when horse and rider are learning something new that they do not get it right. Often in the move off the rider gives too much rein and too strong a leg aid, so the horse puts his head up as he gets a surprise from the legs. Your horse may try to lift up his nose and in doing this he will hollow his back which stops the hind legs coming under properly and it will feel uncomfortable. Feel down the rein during the transition, use your voice to say 'no' and if he pulls against your hands use some leg at the same time to ask him to move forward, feeling on the rein all the time. The moment he starts to respond, stop asking and see if he stays with you, if not, start repeating the aids. Practice makes perfect.

CHANGES OF DIRECTION AND CIRCLES

You can do all the exercises that we covered in the long-reining section: serpentines, loops, diagonals, voltes and figures of eight, lengthening and shortening the gaits and transitions. You can use your imagination to put all the movements together but always double check the manner in which you and your horse are doing them. Always use the half halt to prepare and set your horse up for any movement or to re-balance him, also use your reins bridged all the time.

In the beginning you may need to give the aids more obviously than you would think and possibly move the hands around to help show your horse what you want him to do. As you practise transitions and half halts, so your horse will become better balanced and learn the meaning of the aids. You will, therefore, find that the aids should become finer and softer as

you both know what you are after, which is the ultimate aim.

Whatever exercise you are riding, be it circles or diagonals, always look up to where you are going, know the starting and finishing spot. If you look down, which is a rather common fault and a very easy one to do when training, the weight is altered in the saddle so do be careful to avoid this.

For any changes of direction, turns or circles remember that you should be working your horse with the indirect rein and getting him used to moving away from the pressure. So, two strides before you start a circle, half halt your horse to balance him and make sure you are upright but not tense in the saddle and not putting more weight into one seat bone than the other as this could make your horse move crookedly. Feel on the inside rein to show him the new direction and get a slight bend to the right, then lie the outside rein against the neck. I keep my legs in the same place as when I am going on the straight, that being in the region of the girth area, but I just slightly increase the pressure with the outside lower leg to start the circle. As he settles on to the circle, stop asking with the inside rein and just keep the outside one in place on the neck.

When you want to go on the straight again, about two strides off from your point of finishing, feel on the outside rein and rest the inside one against the neck and say 'straight forward'. If I feel the need I will also use some inside leg. I am then using what is called the lateral aid, inside rein and inside leg.

We all develop our own way of doing things when riding, so you should do what ever you feel best doing, as long as it does not confuse your horse or you! However I believe that the aim is that no one can see your aids.

Possible problem and correction

If you feel at any time that your horse's quarters are slipping out, which means that they are on a different track to the front legs, check that your inside leg is not behind the girth and on too strong, which pushes the quarters out. All you need to do is release your inside leg and make a correction with the outside one; beware of getting your horse swinging from one leg to the other, he must move forward off both equally.

If your horse loses the bend or starts to fall in then take the inside hand closer to the neck but not over, then feeling down the rein at the same time give a little kick with the inside leg and tell him 'out'. Praise him as he does what he is asked but try and work out what caused him to have the problem, by doing this you will learn how to anticipate and prevent them occurring.

STARTING TWO-TRACK WORK

It may surprise you to see that I have included this in this section but it will help keep your horse supple. Even though these movements are worked in both styles some of them for the Western horse are a lead up to specific work.

Instead of going through the explanations of what the movements are as we have already covered them in the long-reining section, I will only give you the names and how to ride them. Whatever work I do with my horses I always ask them to work as correctly as possible, so through all the two-track work I make sure they have the correct bend. You also need to be able to keep your horse straight while doing it, this then helps when you are doing the sidepass work, you learn how to balance and how much to ask and to give when working. I have

included renvers, travers and shoulder-in. Although these three are not used in Western competition they are very good suppling and loosening-up exercises for all horses. Make sure you and your horse are secure in walk then progress to the jog or trot.

SHOULDER-IN

Ride your horse out of the corner, think of going onto a circle, balance him with the half halt, tell him 'steady' and feel on the inside rein to show him the way. Use the outside rein to control the bend and the shoulders. When he brings the shoulders in off the track say 'steady, shoulder'. Balancing him between the reins and leg you now want to ask him to move down the track, so put pressure down onto the inside seat bone and tap him with the inside leg. By releasing your outside leg you have made it very clear in what direction you want him to go, which is down the track. Take your time and make much of him when he has done what you asked. Say 'all right', stop asking with the inside leg, sit level on your seat bones, give equal pressure from both legs and apply the outside rein against the neck, this gives him the aids to walk off into the direction of the bend.

RENVERS

The easiest way to bring your horse into this movement is to do a turn on the haunches, then two strides from the track feel the inside rein to stop him finishing the movement, say 'steady renvers', feel the outside rein to keep the bend and tap him with your inside leg just behind the girth. You will then move down the track, feel on the outside rein to keep the bend and when you want to stop the movement say 'all right', feel on the inside rein to straighten his neck and allow with your outside rein. Have both legs on the girth and give equal pressure to send him off onto a short diagonal. Give him plenty of praise while he is doing the movement and make much when he finishes it.

TRAVERS

Ride through the corner and as you come out of it half halt and feel on the inside rein for the bend. Use the outside rein to control the bend, place the outside leg just behind the girth and tap your horse over with it, ease your inside leg off the girth but be ready to use it if your horse brings his body over too much. Put this all together and as with all the work give your horse the voice aid such as 'steady, travers'. Make much of him and to finish put your inside leg just behind the girth, ease off the outside one and he should straighten up.

As you progress with your lateral work, so you can relate these exercises to each other.

TURN ON THE FOREHAND

Stand your horse square with his nose in a corner and have the reins bridged. To move him off the left leg, feel on the left rein and place the left leg behind the girth, ease off the right leg but it must be ready to be used if he should go to walk

A common problem when starting the full pass is to lose control of the shoulder. In other words it moves too fast and the quarters cannot keep up. Here I am just giving the rider a hand so they get the correct feel of what is wanted.

backwards, the right rein controls the bend and stops him moving forward. At the same time as giving those aids drop some pressure into the left seat bone but do not collapse your body and tell him 'turny'. As he completes the exercise make much of him and ask him to walk on. You can also do this movement at the walk, just half halt to warn him and help to shorten the strides then use exactly the same aids.

TURN ON THE HAUNCHES

This exercise is the lead-in to the roll back and the spin. Walk through a corner and ask your horse to halt as you come out of it – this will help you to control the quarters. Feel the inside rein to show him the direction he will move in and bring the outside rein to the neck but not over, at the same time ease off the inside leg but be ready to use it if he moves back. Place the outside one just in front of the girth, this makes it very clear to your horse it is the front end that

you want to move around. Put everything together, show him the way with the inside rein, the outside one puts pressure on the side of the neck, and tap him with the outside leg not forgetting the voice aid of 'pirouette'. About one stride away from where you decide to finish place your legs in the girth area and apply equal pressure, so on reaching the track he goes straight forward.

You can also do this movement at the walk and it then becomes a walk pirouette. Half halt to shorten the walk, give exactly the same aids and just feel and allow with the reins so you keep him walking through the whole movement.

THE FULL PASS

In this movement you are wanting your horse to move sideways but keep his body parallel with the track that he leaves. When finished training in this exercise he should not progress forward at all as he will be sidepassing over poles eventually.

Stand him up square on the track, feel the inside rein, if needed move the hand away from the neck a little and this will show him the way, keep the outside rein close to the neck. Put pressure into the outside seat bone and place the outside leg on the girth, put all this together at the same time as telling him 'side' and tap him with the outside leg. Take your time, feel on the reins if he goes to move forward, drop your weight into the saddle and say 'no, steady and side'. Remember to release the brakes on your seat. Do only a few steps at a time then ask him to stop, re-balance him, then start again; always give plenty of praise as he is doing the exercise and when he completes it.

THE ROLL BACK AND HOW TO START IT

This is another of the specific movements and one which I consider to be basic. I am sure that you will have seen your horse galloping, stopping dead and turning back over his haunches and moving off again; this is the essence of the roll back. Take your horse somewhere you have something solid you can aim at, such as a fence. As you have already done the turn on the haunches, you and your horse will have an understanding of this movement. You could jog slowly at the fence and just in front of it drop your weight down into the saddle and say 'stop'. As soon as he stops you want to bring the front end round as quickly as possible but the back end must not move out. Put the outside rein to the neck, lead him round with the inside rein, release your inside leg but have your outside one on just behind the girth. When he comes round, move straight off into trot again and make a big fuss of him. The aim is to canter, stop, do the roll back and canter out again. Practise this little and often as it is very important for both of you to learn it. Remember to give your horse encouragement and the words for movement during the whole exercise and of course finish with praise.

THE REIN BACK

Having practised this on the ground I hope I am right in believing that you and your horse can now do this as required. When riding, halt your horse square, make sure that you are sitting with your weight balanced in the saddle. To ask your horse to come back, feel on both reins, tell him

As you can see Idolo can do a roll back quite easily without a rider on board, note the flexion through his hocks.

'back, steady' and move your lower legs just behind the girth but do not squeeze, only rest them on his sides. The moment he responds, stop the rein aid but keep the others on, then ask him to 'halt': immediately release all the backing aids, drop the weight into your seat and close the knees and say 'halt', giving him a lot of praise. Then close your legs, ease the hands and ask him to 'walk on' for a few strides. Halt again and repeat the rein back aids including the voice. Ask for only one step at a time initially. As he responds go for more but always slowly and halt after each step, this way you can always control your horse's movement.

This rider is doing this for the first time, it is good that she is allowing Hans to look down where he is going, maybe the reins could have been just a little longer then she would not have her arms stretched forward so much, but overall a good picture.

You will see why you need this in the trail section.

If for any reason he will not go back do not fight him but settle him down. If you can, get someone to stand beside his shoulder and, while you give all the aids, they should tap him on the front leg until he moves back away from the irritant. The minute he moves make a big fuss and give him a reward. Do this a few times then leave it and try a couple of times on the other rein, do this for a few days and he will understand what is wanted. If you are on your own make sure your horse will do it from the floor for you when asked by tapping him on the

top of the leg and at the same time telling him 'back'. When you are riding him, put the reins in one hand and tap him again in the same place as you did from the floor, make much of him as he makes any move backwards.

A word of warning, if you are going to compete make sure that you know all the terminology. I made a hiccup at an indoor show in a riding class. I was very pleased with the way my horse was going then the steward said 'riders reverse'. I thought that he meant halt and rein back, which I promptly did! This was much to the embarrassment of my father who covered his eyes as I caused a mini pile up. 'Reverse' means change the direction. Still, I took it in good humour when the other riders started making comments about dressage riders not knowing the directions.

TRAIL OBSTACLES

These obstacles are in reality worth practising even if you only hack out English or Western.

In competition there are standard requirements that always have to be met and most of them are covered below. The fun thing however is that really you can do whatever you want with your horse. With all new things that you are introducing your horse to, do not rush but talk to him and let him know that everything is all right, let him look and if necessary walk quietly around on both reins. Some horses get even more confidence if you walk over first and let them follow you or have another horse whom they can follow and gain confidence from.

THE GATE

I think this is the most common obstacle you will come across and for all horses of any age it is a particularly good exercise for them to practise. Now you will see one of the reasons for teaching your horse the two-track work, not only for suppling but as a necessity for assisting both of you in going sideways.

Stand parallel with the gate so that you can undo the latch easily, do not let the gate go, ask your horse to back up so that he can then do a quarter turn on the haunches, keep your outside leg (the one away from the gate) just behind the girth and rest the outside rein against the neck. Tell him whatever word you use (I would say 'pirouette') and you must still be holding the gate. Make sure you release the inside leg next to the gate, this makes it very clear to your horse that he can move his shoulders that way, if he goes to move his quarters say 'no' and touch him with the leg he is pushing towards to stop him moving them. Take your time, do not rush and do one step at a time. When there is enough space for you both to walk through, proceed still holding the gate and sliding your hand forward to the latch end. When level with your knee, still holding the gate, ask your horse to do a turn on the forehand, then sidepass to close the gate and put the latch down. Ask your horse to wait and not just move off as soon as he thinks it is all right. It is quicker to do this exercise, than to write about how to do it! I think this is the safest way to handle a gate.

THE BRIDGE

We covered the introduction to noises in Part 2 when working on the ground. If you did not do

Open the latch and rein back . . .

quarter turn on haunches and walk forward . . .

followed by quarter turn on forehand . . .

then sidepass and back if needed . . .

secure gate

it then go back and do your homework, as the noise from the hollow wooden bridge may worry your horse in the beginning.

Walk slowly up to the bridge and ask him to 'stop' just in front of it, feel on the reins and then give the contact to allow your horse to drop his head down to look and smell the bridge. I would also ask him to look down by giving him another little aid, I scratch his neck by the withers. Tell him to walk on and over, add some pressure with your legs and be ready to stop him walking sideways if he is not sure. He just might test it by placing a foot on it, praise him and say 'all right, walk on!' After he has done this a few times and as he gets used to the noise then ask him to stand still and wait. Make a fuss of him when he does this. In the beginning I would put some bales of straw on each side of the bridge just to help guide my horse over.

SIDEPASSING OVER POLES

Even though I have always done the full pass with my horses as I find it a useful training and loosening-up exercise, I also use it in my displays. I would categorise the sidepass as a specific Western movement. I am sure that after you have worked through this exercise a few times, you will feel the benefit of being able to move your horse around and to place him where you wish.

Sidepassing is a fine balancing act between the hands and legs because, too much contact on the reins and he will go backwards, not enough and he will move forward. Practise will help you to learn to judge the feel you need in this exercise. If you put a leg in front or behind the girth you are asking one end or the other to move. A leg on the girth is the aid for the whole body to move.

Pick up and bridge the reins. If you are moving to the left you need to place some weight into the right seat bones, remember not to twist or turn your body, and apply the pressure with the right leg on the girth. To allow movement to happen you must take your left leg away from the body. Keep an even feel on both reins and, at the same time as giving the other aids, give your voice aid of 'side'. Try to keep the pole in the middle of your horse's legs, go only a few strides at a time then ask him to halt and make a fuss of him. Carry on when ready. The aids are reversed if you are moving to the right.

Try this exercise before doing the T exercise. Put two poles in a straight line with a gap of about eight feet (2.5m) between them. Stand your horse square and ask him to wait. Sidepass over the first one then prepare for a quarter turn on the haunches. Give a half halt with the outside rein, say 'steady' and ask him around with the inside rein and place the outside rein against his neck making sure he looks in the direction he is going in. Put your outside leg a little forward and tap him with the inside of your heel and, at the same time, tell him 'turny'. You now need to do a quarter turn on the forehand. Give a feel on the outside rein, this rein controls the bend and stops him walking forward. Put your outside leg behind the girth and tap him with your heel, at the same time tell him 'turny'. Whilst your horse has changed position, he is moving in the same direction. When you complete it give him plenty of praise, then ask him to move on down the next pole. At the end of the exercise make much of him.

Now proceed to do the broken T exercise. Place one pole on the ground then put two more at one end so that they form a broken T shape.

Floribunda is starting the full pass to the left, note that I have moved my left leg away to allow her to move the way I am asking.

Now I am bringing her round into a turn on the haunches to the left . . .

we carry on sidepassing to the left and at the end we halt then come back to the right . . .

followed by a turn on the forehand to the right, she has a little too much bend in her neck on this one. . .

finishing with a sidepass to the right.

I am just looking to check that we are not too close to the boards to start the turn.

Floribunda has just raised her head a little so I am feeling down the rein with my fingers to get her attention back before I continue.

You can see that the reins are loose and she is going back well, but it is a pity that I am looking down!

Make sure that the three ends do not touch, you will see the reason why in a minute.

Stand by the top right end of the T with the poles on your left, stand your horse square and ask him to wait.

Sidepass to the end of the first pole. As you reach the end, you need to make a quarter turn on the haunches to the left through the gap, now sidepass down this pole, to the end. Reposition yourself and ask your horse to go sideways to the right, to the end of the pole. You now do a quarter turn on the forehand to the right and sidepass down the next pole. At the end of the exercise, make much of him.

THE TURNAROUND

Do not confuse this movement with the spin, which is when the horse pivots and spins round very fast on one hind leg – that is an advanced training movement. Both these movements are specific to Western. Out of all the exercises I have covered in this section, the turnaround is one I have to admit that I had never done until I started competitive Western riding. On the other hand, some riders do half this movement without realising it if they ride a walk pirouette badly.

This is a useful exercise which will show you how much control you have over your horse's body. Make a square with four poles, start with it the length of your horse's body and as he progresses make it smaller. The idea is that he should step in to the box without touching a pole. Give him his aid to drop his head and look where he is going once in, we want him to do what I call a turn on the belly. I stay in the same spot as if I am pinned to the floor like a carousel

horse but my horse's quarters and shoulders move around and complete a full 360 degree turn.

To do this to the left, feel on the left rein so he looks in the correct direction and lean the outside rein against the neck, put the left leg back a little and bring the right one forward. Give the aids at the same time and give him a voice aid, it is best to do only a few steps at a time and make them slow and short. Do a few then stop, praise him and repeat this until you have done the whole movement. When you finish, halt, close your legs, feel the rein and ask him to drop his nose down to look where he is going and walk on out of the box.

ANY PROBLEMS

By now you should know the routine if you have a problem: take your time and analyse it. I am confident that you will be able to work it out and remember it is all about thinking riding. Always do the movements on both reins and be satisfied with a few steps to start then progress slowly and keep your reins bridged in all the work until secure, then try neck reining.

REIN BACK ON THE CIRCLE

I find that there are some interesting comparisons between English and Western styles. Put two horses of both styles together and one would think how different they were because they would not look the same. However our objectives run parallel. In our own way and presentation we are working towards the same goals – lightness, ease of work and self-

carriage. This movement illuminates one of the comparisons. We all train our horses to go back yet I cannot think of any competition that includes this movement, certainly not dressage. For some reason many riders will only train their horses to move back in a straight line, I personally find this a useful exercise in co-ordination as well as moving the horse's muscles in a different way. You can also check to see if your horse is on the aids.

Stand your horse up square at the start of the circle. Ask him to 'back, slowly' then move the outside leg back just behind the girth. Keep the rein pressure equal and make sure the inside leg is away from his side so you are letting the quarters come round. Ask him to halt and make much of him then continue and finish the circle.

REIN BACK THROUGH A COMPLEX

You can also back up through an L-shaped complex. Ride forward through it then halt, feel the reins, close your legs and ask him to back up. This is another exercise which I have not seen at any shows apart from Western shows. The more advanced you and your horse get at this exercise then you can make it harder, I tend to start with the poles raised. Wherever you put them initially keep them wide apart and as you progress, bring them closer together. Go slowly, a step at a time and stop just before the corner, you need to think of working your way around the corner. Drop your weight onto your outside seat bone and he should move his quarters away from the pressure, you may need to feel on the outside rein to help balance him through the turn. Do one step then release your aids and stop, move off again and re-apply the aids. Once

you complete the turn ask him to halt and wait, then slowly back up out of the complex. Halt at the end and make much of him.

SUMMING UP

I hope that you find these exercises helpful for both you and your horse as well as being motivated to go and have a go at Western work. It is worth going to see the shows, I really like watching the cutting horses work. You can see them reading those cows; both will have their heads down, eyeballing each other. The riders sit very quietly and let the horses carry out the work; those horses really have another sense – rather like a sheepdog I think.

...AND FINALLY

I would not be so naïve or bold as to say I know all the answers but with the help of all the animals I am still learning.

I saw a French trainer and stuntman on video who affirmed my thoughts by saying 'never make training a secret, because it is for the good of the horse that the word should be spread'.

Remember above all else that what we do with any horse is by his consent. Never try to get him so submissive that he loses the spark for life, do not abuse his trust and confidence. Working with any animal is all about cooperation not domination. He should always be happy to see you.

I hope you have enjoyed going through this book and that you will try some New Sensations with your equine friend. Good luck.

Enjoy your horse, have a great life . . .

VOCABULARY

In order to help you extend your word range I have written out my words with their meanings. It is so important to remember that you can train your horse in any language, literally he learns what you teach him.

A very real problem, that many people do not even think about when they buy a horse from a foreign country, is that the horse only understands that language and basically has no idea what the new language is that is being spoken, so he has to learn it.

Yes it is debatable as to whether or not horses understand the words, I believe they do. However, the tone used is very important when talking to your horse: keep it soft and always draw out the second syllable, only use a stronger tone to reprimand.

MY WORDS	THEIR MEANING
Allez	more energy needed
All right	signal he can stop what he is doing
Back	back up or rein back
Canter	three-time pace
Catch	catching an object when thrown
Change	changing direction in front of you
Close	close a gate with nose or chest
Come here	come when called
Forward	when you want him to go straight
Good boy	words of praise
Halt	halt from movement
Head down	asking him to drop his head

MY WORDS	THEIR MEANING
His name	must know his name
Kneel down	going down on one knee
Leave	if he keeps trying to pick up something not wanted
Left lift	left leg for Spanish Walk
Lie down	lying down
Listen	get his attention
No	stop it
Open	open gate with nose or chin
Out	when the horse is falling in
Pick up hold	holds any object you point to
Pirouette	full 360 degree turn
Place	he goes to the place you point to
Push	pushing anything
Renvers	quarters to the wall
Right lift	right leg for Spanish Walk
Shoulder	shoulder in
Slowly	walking slowly
Stand	stand after halt
Side	sideways movement, full pass
Stay	stay in position
Steady	slow down
Step over	stepping over obstacles
Stretch	stretching out forelegs and dropping shoulders
Travers	quarters in
Trot	two-time pace
Turny	turn on the forehand
Undo	untie a knot or the like
Wait	until given a new request
Walk	four-time pace
Yes	he nods his head up and down

USEFUL ADDRESSES

British Driving Society
27 Dugard Place
Barford
Nr Warwick
Warwickshire CV35 8DX

British Horse Driving Trials Association
Dykelands Farm
Whenby
York YO6 4SP

Riding for the Disabled Association
Avenue R
National Agricultural Centre
Stoneleigh
Kenilworth
Warwickshire CV8 2LY

Western Equestrian Society
20 Newlands Close
Yateley
Surrey GU17 7HE

Western Horsemen's Association of
Great Britain
Llamedoes
The Clumps
Ashford
Middlesex TW15 1AT

Mark Davies Injured Riders Fund
Little Woolpit
Ewhurst
Cranleigh
Surrey GU6 7NP

International League for the Protection of
Horses
Anne Colvin House
Snetterton
Norwich
Norfolk NR16 2LR

British Equestrian Vaulting
47 Manderley Close
Easton Green
Coventry CV5 7NR

Tanya Larrigan
Maywood Stud
Frogs Hole Lane
Woodchurch
Ashford Kent
TN26 3QZ
Tel: 01233 860076
Fax: 01233 860103
www.tanyashorses.com